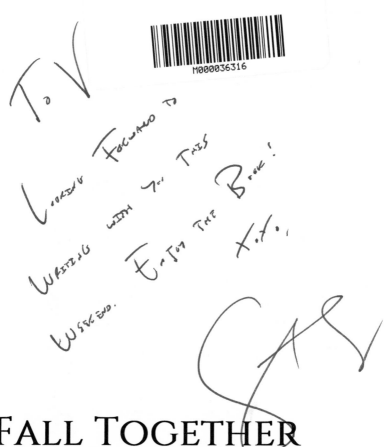

To V

Looking Forward To
Writing with You This
Weekend. Enjoy The Book!
Xoxo,

FALL TOGETHER
BY SARAH ANNE STRICKLEY

Sarah Anne Strickley's stunning debut collection features a long list of memorable characters, survivors of some disasters and creators of others, and those barely hanging on who stubbornly hang on nonetheless and sometimes triumph. In several stories the mundane slips into the mysterious as gracefully as it does in the work of Angela Carter or Aimee Bender, while other stories are more realistic, mournful elegies revealing lives where tragedy swallows some and liberates others. All are shot through with beautiful prose, startling imagery, and a wicked sense of humor, and all investigate the truly important things, the price we pay and the rewards we reap to be that most mystifying of creatures: bewildered, bedeviled, and yet resilient.

~Paul Griner,
author of *Hurry Please I Want to Know*

I could not stop reading these strange, sometimes savage, always revelatory tales. Sarah Anne Strickley takes us from coal mine to front porch to trashed riverbank with a daring that had me holding my breath. Part poet, part sorceress, and every part seer—and we're the lucky ones who get to discover her.

~Anna Solomon,
author of *Leaving Lucy Pear*

There's enormous power in these sharp, vivid stories about people who try and fail to conceal their faults and desires. Strickley renders her characters' sorrow and longing with such force I had to put the book down between stories to recover. Each story in this collection is a marvel of intelligence and empathy.

~Leah Stewart,
author of *What You Don't Know About Charlie Outlaw*

FALL TOGETHER

CONTENTS

For Ian, who always believed

THE ART PROFESSOR'S GUIDE TO MYSTICAL PREGNANCY

1. *Conception*

Once the idea arrived in her mind, Amelia was convinced: she was pregnant. On some level, of course, she knew this was impossible. She was a single woman who loved women. And even if she had chanced to find someone with whom to start a family, menopause had begun very early for her—in her early thirties—and childbearing was surely out of the question for her now at fifty-five. Still, she could not shake her mind's ironclad certainty: she was pregnant. Pregnant with what, she did not know, but she was sure of it. *If it is a child*, she thought, *it's a strange and doomed little being. It's a thing that attached itself to a wall years ago and grew unnoticed like a mold.*

Was it a child? The last time she had sex with a man, she was in her early thirties and he was her ex-husband, Warren. She remembered him as dusky around the chin when it happened, the distant gaze of the haunted soldier in his eyes. These days he was a successful painter with a gaggle of children and two subsequent ex-wives. She imagined calling him at this late date with the news that the thing they'd done, so distant as to be a mere glint of memory—the smell of the coats on the mattress where he'd leaned into her, the view of her tan pantyhose stretched between her knees—had resulted in the world's most persistent fetus.

"We're expecting!" she'd say.

"Expecting what?" he'd say.

So, perhaps it wasn't a child, but it occupied her as a child might occupy its mother. It sat large and low and round in her belly, and it grew. It needed her in a way that she found pleasing enough to rationalize resisting the idea of inviting doctors to weigh in on the situation. Medicine had only served to embarrass her in the past. The early onset of menopause was caused by a tumor sitting like a frozen dime on her pituitary gland and went undiagnosed and misdiagnosed for a quite a long time. And so, despite her physician's annual check-up reminder in her mailbox, she told no one about the strange presence in her uterus.

2. *The First Trimester*

It wasn't difficult to hide things about herself. She withdrew from her quiet social life on the excuse of home improvement efforts. Her garage was filled with weathered stones and rusted slabs of metal. She told her friends on the art history faculty that she intended to blow off a little professorial steam by transforming the materials into an art display at the end of her drive. But, instead of tending to these healthy ambitions, she took long baths in the evening and marveled at her own expansion, her belly rising from the chalked bergamot water like an atoll. She stood naked in the square bathroom mirror and thought of Thomas Eakins and his nude photographic studies, how the clothing would drape if she were to be painted as a Madonna or a grieving saint. She adjusted her yoga poses to accommodate the new weight in her middle, letting it settle over her elastic waistband.

Soon her sleep came under the influence of her expanding belly. She dreamed regularly of birthing a red, sequined shape. It would tow her to the bottom of a sea in which she could somehow breathe. She and the shape would reach the sand and make a pleasing impression in its softness. They would nap together, consider movement, and then nap again. Nothing was pressing in these dreams. The sea tilted her gently and her hair rose above her head like a dirty blonde plant. She was happy.

She'd never perused the maternity section in the department store before, but now that the idea of birth was with her and now that her clothing no longer fit in her middle, she felt compelled to visit. She was appalled by the options available to expectant mothers. The clothes seemed meant to infantilize the woman, to turn her into the baby. Perhaps this protected her from the advances of men, she thought. It would be like child molestation, touching a woman in sleeves so pink and puffed. Little daisy and bunny print bra and panty sets. Of course, that didn't stop the child molesters, did it?

At an expensive boutique in the city, she found what seemed to be a targeted response to the chain-store offerings. Low-waisted lingerie and elastisized business blouses in which the cleavage was meant to sit like an offering above the belly. *I am fertile*, these clothes seemed to say. *Deal with it*. She landed upon maternity blue jeans with a large elastic middle where the button and zipper would normally reach. They were so soft, and the angle of the pockets was more stylish than that of any of the other slacks she owned. She worried the salesgirl might question her. *Why would you need a pair of pants like these?* But instead she nodded her head approvingly and said, "Good choice."

The unvarnished truth: Amelia felt younger in these jeans. She imagined herself leaning over a billiard table to shoot a ball while wearing them, something she'd never dreamed of doing before. If anyone noticed they were pregnancy pants—someone who was even remotely familiar with the circumstances of her life, for example—she'd have far too much explaining to do, so she wore them with long, bulky sweaters, regretting the disappearance of the jaunty pockets into the folds of wool. It was enough sometimes just to rest her hands in the small of her back and know that they were there to send a thrill up her spine.

She spent the second month accommodating the changes in her body. Rolling with them. She was able to admit that she was enjoying herself, though she knew she shouldn't. She knew she should be worried. But she felt so safe with her heavy belly sitting in her lap while she slept on her side. *Come on, let's get up,* she said to herself—and it—when she woke in the morning. *Let's have something to eat,* she said. *Let's head in to work. Let's take a break. Let's enjoy the nice shift in the weather, shall we?*

She allowed her hands to move absently toward her belly when they weren't otherwise occupied. They often stroked the round shape, as though to comfort it, and she found the movement to be quite comforting herself. She could see why expectant mothers were forever fondling their midriffs, like there were magnets inside their palms and the babies inside were powerful metals. It had been a long time since she'd touched this part of her body, or any, with the gentleness and care she now found perfectly natural and fitting.

When she began to feel a certain tension, a stinging heat rippling through, she suspected their days together were numbered. She hoped she could hold on until the last days of spring. At least then she'd have the summer months to recover from whatever procedure the doctors would perform on her—call it a C-section, call it a surgery. In the meantime, she fell into a stubborn intransigence. She had no wish to die, but neither did she wish for the idea of the being inside of her to perish. She made a half-witted deal with herself: it was a real pregnancy until someone called her out on her lapse into fantastical thinking. Let someone else introduce logic and ruin the fun. It was silly way to make a decision, the kind of reasoning a toddler might execute while indulging the habitual theft of candies, but what else was there? No one gives you a guidebook on impossible miracle pregnancies. And even if there were a guidebook for such a thing, Amelia's body would be the one to disobey all expectations.

Exhibit A: the tumor that sat at the bottom of her brain through so many difficult years had caused Amelia to lactate at the age of seventeen, still a virgin and in her first year of college. It secreted a hormone called prolactin, stopped her periods, decimated her sex drive, and brought milk into her breasts. Her doctor said it was related to the birth control she was taking and frowned. He phoned her mother and asked her if she was aware that her daughter was sexually active, as it was his obligation as an employee of the state to inform on minors.

Amelia was removed from the state school and dropped into a private institution for women in a piney northern state. It was a punishment meant to remove her of her wanton desires for men, but she'd only sought the birth control from the campus clinic because she'd been embarrassed in the dorms by a pack of girls who'd collectively deemed her queer. She took the pill conspicuously in school, so as to remove herself from suspicion, complaining (though she'd hardly ever talked at all before) about how hardhardhard it was to remember when to take it, how unfair it was that men didn't have to remember when to take pills.

That she'd been punished for her trickery with breasts that carried the weight of birth had not surprised her. She was a superstitious and cynical sort of girl. That she'd been punished for her sexual leanings with a world replete of arduous young women came as a bit of a shock, but not for the reasons one might expect. She had no trouble finding women to love and even less trouble finding women to love her—hers was an astringent beauty, as sharp and clear as her mind—but rather it was the rest that confounded her. She had sex but she didn't enjoy it, didn't feel it. It was an intellectual gesture; her body was disinterested. A mere sputter of feel was all she could seem to muster. She knew to expect more. But it was the kind of absence for which many subsequent doctors told her she should be thankful. *Have a glass of wine*, they told her. *Read a book on the couch. Adopt pets.* It was the tumor, of course, but no one thought to look beneath her brain for the problem.

After trying and failing again and again with women, she'd married Warren and tried for five years to affect a happy marriage through wardrobe selection and recipes. It didn't work, and he didn't hold it against her. He was the type to amble through life amiably; it was all one big learning experience for him, with no rules and few obligations worth meeting. When they divorced, Amelia decided to be happy she wasn't like the rest of them, the lust-addled fools, and settled into a very peaceful and resigned way of living, a life empty of desire's complications and drama.

She was often very lonely, but that's just the way she was. There wasn't anything to be done about it. The fact that she was very smart helped. She won the most prestigious position in her field by phoning and asking for it. One perk of the job was career-long use of a cottage that looked like a half-capped mushroom on a lovely grey cape. She lived alone there happily for twenty years. And then—Exhibit B—she met a team of doctors who told her it had all been a mistake. "We need to re-evaluate your physiological trajectory," they said. She signed the papers and submitted to a battery of tests, some simple and some involving suites of ticking machinery and equipment.

When the tumor was discovered, she proved a less interesting specimen than initially expected. Small-town hacks with little more than stethoscopes in their arsenals could have diagnosed her properly if they'd been able to get past the idea that she was just your average disinterested female. The surgery removed both the culprit tissue and the cause of her solitude in a matter of hours. She was given a booklet, one that described pictorially the decimation of her vaginal folds. With hormonal therapy, she might achieve a modicum of feeling, but sex would never be entirely pleasurable. *Embrace your feeling*, the doctors told her now. *Get to know yourself. Adopt pets.* She chose the most intense hormonal regimen available in North America and went into it at a desperate keel.

It had come as no surprise, really, when she felt the new thing growing in her belly. She understood it as a response, a reaction. Maybe it wasn't a child, but it was the product of an affair of sorts, a lifelong fling with a body that refused to obey organic logic. At least that was the metaphor she finally determined to apply to it. She knew it wasn't right, that the comparison was an indulgence, but she wasn't strong enough to fight its influence on her thinking. She needed to be saved.

Her strategy of self-isolation was more effective than she expected. No one knocked, no one called. She maintained social niceties by e-mail. *Sorry I missed you at the fundraiser! Let's catch up when the weather turns!* While she awaited intervention, she watched knitting tutorials online. She had no intention of making pink or blue baby booties, but now she'd know how to do it if it turned out she wasn't insane. She also researched the politics of breastfeeding and babywearing and vaccination and decided she stood somewhere in the middle—not a granola witch goddess, but not a homeschooling harpy. It was easy to get pulled into all sorts of controversies when expecting. She endeavored to reserve judgment. It was how she'd want to behave if she were to encounter mothers on the playground or the grocery. Lord knows they'd have reason to judge her.

3. *The Second Trimester*

She wasn't overly hungry, but when she swallowed food, it seemed not to fit. Her arms and legs and face began to thin. She found the change in the mirror exciting. Her persistent double chin, the thing a resentful colleague had once called a *gizzard*, meaning a *wattle*, had all but vanished. The flesh that shook beneath her arms when she used the blackboard to teach was tighter to the bone. She could see the muscle she'd always known was there beneath the fat when she flexed. She felt sinuous and stronger. She wore size XXXL sweatshirts to cover her belly's bulk and black tights to show off her new legs, which she crossed and uncrossed with new energy. Before, she had to settle for an ankle flung atop a knee, but now she could almost achieve the double cross—at the knee and the ankle both, the most elegant position the female form could take in a chair.

Still, no one mentioned her bulbous belly. The silence was almost disconcerting. Weren't women forever complaining about the free license others took with assessments of their bodies? Weren't they always fighting off the judgment encased inside little compliments and insults? *You look like you've lost weight. Are you sure* veganism *isn't another word for* eating disorder? Where was the choir of uninvited opinions she'd been led to expect by the feminist blogs? As the weeks passed, she allowed herself to consider the possibility that the spell was powerful enough to enchant others. Maybe the thing inside her was exerting a power that extended beyond the confines of her womb. Maybe she was the host of a beacon of warm companionability, a strobing judgment-free zone.

Then a student in one of her classes called her out. "You're getting skinny-fat," she said. "That's what happened to me when I was a freshman."

"What are you talking about?" said Amelia. Her heart went wild—a caught animal in a bone cage. The girl, one whose name she only half-knew, Laura or Lindsay, said it was beer. "When you drink the cheap stuff, it's what happens," she said.

"You think I drink cheap beer?" she asked.

The girl looked confused and then laughed. "No," she said. "I guess you wouldn't."

Each knew something about the other then. The girl was the type vain enough to assume everyone was like her and her professor was the type self-consumed and crazy enough to believe no one saw her grotesque transformation. But one had more power than the other.

"I guess I don't know what I'm talking about," said the girl. "I'll see you next week in class."

Amelia had made an agreement with herself—as soon as someone noticed, it was time to wake up—and she was hesitant to go back on an agreement, but she'd never trusted a student's perception before and she didn't know why she should start now. Her students were always so wrong about her. They assumed she didn't know how to use computers, and they assumed she didn't watch films or television or listen to music, and they assumed she was a lonely widow and all because she was an older woman, an unmarried eccentric. It may have been this girl or another one exactly like her who had told her earlier in the semester that she didn't see why they had to think about the art they talked about in class. "I mean, that's the whole point of art, isn't it?" she'd said. "You don't have to think."

That night she sat in the beached rowboat that had always been with the house and watched the sun set itself down in the water. Her cat stayed with her for a few hours and then vanished into the weeds. When it was dark enough that she could imagine her body was as it always had been, without the fact of herself to remind her of the changes, she found that she could still sense her girth without seeing or touching it. It was a red ball, a perfectly spherical shape. There was nothing anatomical about it. Its sheen was elegiac, the radiating brilliance of layered ruby sequins, and there was a lyric stillness about it, a tranquility. Yet, if you opened her up to look inside, there'd be nothing much to see, no poetry. Some kinds of beauty are like that, she supposed, like blood. When you expose it to the air, it dulls considerably.

When she woke, she found that she was adrift in the boat. It was morning and somehow she'd been sailing;

she didn't know how long. There were slick leeches affixed to her arms and legs, and her hands were waterlogged, as though she'd been using them too long to paddle, but she had no memory of movement. It was a struggle getting to shore and then grasping and pulling each leech as she stood in the knee-high weeds was no picnic, but it was her figure reflected in the long glass widows of her house that finally tipped her into panic. She looked like something washed up dead and bloated. Grey.

A few years after she'd moved to the cape, they'd pulled a man out of it. He'd been hiking in the nearby woods and become lost. He was dead for a week before anyone noticed he was gone. It wasn't the saddest thing Amelia had ever heard, but it disturbed her. For weeks, she'd thought of him dying so near her house. He might have seen her kitchen lights and moved toward them, found the deepest part of the water instead. Now, looking at herself in the glass, she worried she'd gone too far. Maybe she should seek a second opinion.

The rest of the faculty played dumb when she confronted them about it. "Do I look OK to you?" she asked. "Tell me the truth. I can handle it."

"Of course," they said.

"I don't look sick?" she asked. "Or maybe pregnant?" she risked.

"No," they assured her. "You look fantastic."

They were her friends, the people with whom she most frequently spoke, and they'd always claimed a certain stake in her private life. When her first cat had died, for example, they bought her another, leaving it complete with name and tag (Victorine, 2774 Albey Way), in her office for her to find, and they always phoned her when any drinking or griping was afoot. Surely they would tell her if something was awry. "One of my students called me skinny-fat," she said. She pressed her oversized sweater to her belly to reveal its contours. "That can't be good, can it?"

The department head, an ancient German, asked Amelia what she expected. "How old are you?" he asked. "You were thinking you'd always be a girl?" Amelia had never thought of herself as girlish, but this seemed beside the point. "When my sister had the change in life, she said, 'My husband will no longer love me.' I told her, no marriage is for love," he said. He reached into the shelf behind him and gave her a book of translated verse. *Dichter und Dichterin.* "Talk to someone you despise," he said. "Someone who hates you."

But there was no one to hate or love. If she had a mother, she supposed, she would call her. This was the kind of thing you shared with your mother. But her mother was long dead, and they'd never spoken openly. The only time Amelia felt a warmth for family was when she saw how she felt things were supposed to be on television—a confession she only begrudgingly made to herself and one she had only once made to someone else. "I'm envious of the dysfunctional families on sitcoms," she'd told her therapist. "They have boundaries to cross. We have nothing between us." She didn't like to admit that she was lured easily by the notion of a better way, the flawed but perfect family. She had a brother, but he was much younger, the product of her estranged father's second marriage, and he seemed interested only in knowing if she intended to make claims on their father's estate, which amounted to nothing but a Corvette Stingray in a self-storage unit.

In the end, she called her ex-husband, who'd at least been her family in the institutional sense, and left him a slightly misleading voicemail. She wanted to entice his curiosity without seeming, really, to require his assistance. Otherwise, he might not return her call. She was flip, mock-serious. "Warren," she said. "How are you? I wonder if you could help us resolve a bit of debate we're having."

He called back immediately and she answered without thinking.

"You've got my interest," he said.

"Were you screening calls?"

"Initially," he said, "but then I couldn't get to the button fast enough. I'm at the park with the kids."

She knew instantly where he was and could picture it quite clearly. They'd lived only a block from this park when they were married and he lived there now with two of his five children and a nanny who, according to the gossip, had lately become a girlfriend. In their younger, married days, Amelia and Warren had played on the slides and monkey bars together as though they were the children they both knew they'd never have. He once sat on a thick bed of mulch and solemnly confessed to her that he knew she was leaving him. She didn't have the courage to lie to him, but she'd been nice. She didn't point out his affairs or his failure to love anyone nearly as much as he loved himself. "Yes, but I'm leaving very slowly," she said. "You won't even notice when I'm gone."

"What's the debate and who's having it?" he asked now.

She knew she couldn't summon the flirty tone she'd manufactured within the hollow privacy of his voicemail account. "Do you want to call me back later?" she asked.

"I have five minutes before I have to haul these kids to their mothers' for dinner and then I don't know what's happening."

"It's a little complicated," she said. "I don't know if I can explain it in five minutes."

"What's the gist?"

"Children."

"What about them?"

She forced words out, knowing he'd mistake her stuttering for the strain of impromptu summarization. "I don't know. The whole concept of them," she said.

"That does sound complicated. Who's having the debate?"

"What's the difference?"

"It would give me a context," he said. "Is it that Clare woman? Connie?"

"I haven't talked to Connie in ten years," she said. "I haven't thought of her in just as long."

"How long has it been since we talked?"

"Warren," she said. "I think there's something wrong with me."

"Oh," he said. He was surprised. She could hear it in the tone of the word, the long vowel. He'd expected to be invited into some kind of airy intellectual wrangling but now he was involved in something else. "Like, *medically* wrong?" he asked.

"Maybe. Probably. I don't trust anyone to tell me the truth, or I don't want to hear the truth, or we're not actually talking and I'm in a strange dream or one of your depressing paintings."

"Can you travel?" he asked. "I'm in the studio a lot these days."

"I was hoping you'd come down."

"I'll call you when I know what's possible."

She heard children squealing on the playground and the motor of a plane, flying low. He sighed and then he was gone. The lectures she gave in the week that followed were on *horror vacui*. Translated literally it was the fear of emptiness, but it was also a kind of outsider art that had gained popularity among young artists who were striving to draw comparisons between the crazed artistic compulsions of jailed mental patients and the modern urban landscape of reaching billboards and flashing lights. Her belly sunk low, and she made no effort to conceal it. A rim of chalk gathered on its underside when she wrote on the board.

When young women raised their hands in response to her questions—they all looked like Lauras or Lindsays to her now and so she could bring herself to call on none of them—she ignored them. Her ire was not gender-specific. When male hands arrived in the mess, she pointed and then didn't wait for the response to reveal the answer. "We can re-inscribe," she said, apropos of nothing, when they tried to argue with her. "Filling space can become a celebration, rather than a compulsion." Students, both men and women, complained about her to the German. She was manhandling them, they said. She was supposed to be the nice one on the faculty, approachable. Were their grades going to be affected? The German told her to take a week off; he'd cover her classes. And so now she was completely isolated. Call it maternal confinement, call it administrative leave.

4. *The Third Trimester*
At home, she developed new methods of swallowing. She set a bit of bread on a finger and leaned it in. She bathed with the water higher. The bulge was now leaning to the left. It was becoming something different. Not entirely round. At first, it had felt so comfortable and warm, the fullness after a meal. And then it became a burden. It wanted more room. It shoved things out of the way. She

imagined her heart inside her chest. A weak muscle wound round with her displaced bowels.

By the time Warren appeared in her backyard, standing without a word beside her as she sat in her beached boat, she had given over to the idea that the thing growing inside her was going to kill her and that it was all completely fitting. The perfect end to the perfect lack of a true beginning. He took her hand in his and shook it. "You're wearing fancy jeans," he said.

"They're from a maternity boutique," she said. "They're very stylish."

"I see that."

The cape was more yellow than grey in the light of the setting sun, and the leaves were sitting lush on the trees surrounding the water like offerings about to drop.

"What do you want to do?" she asked.

"I want to drink like a fish and I want you to drink like a fish with me, but those days are long gone. We'll have to settle for sitting on your couch and sharing some awkward silences. You do have a couch, don't you? Or, have you forsaken that comfort too?"

"I have a couch," she said. "I'm not insane."

They sat in her living room, one on each of her two cream-colored settees. The coffee table set between them was one piece of many she'd made herself out of driftwood pulled from the cape. She'd mounted a clear slab of glass above the knots of weathered branches. Warren toed a streak on the glass with a bare foot. "You hate it when people do this, don't you?" he said. "You're already thinking about getting out the glass cleaner when I go to the bathroom."

"No," she said. "I'm thinking about putting that thing back in the water where I found it. I'm thinking about putting everything in there."

"If you're going to be like this, we may need coffee," he said.

He stretched his long legs and stalked into the kitchen, where he slammed cupboards and rifled through drawers. He knew where she liked to keep things, but he was making a fuss because he wanted her to know what kind of risk he was taking by talking to her. Not insubstantial. He had problems of his own that often threatened to overwhelm him and he didn't need hers. Of course, there were risks for her, as well. Warren didn't play around with words. You called him when you wanted the truth, which was never nice and never pretty and came at a price. When he returned with the coffee press and cups, balanced on a ridiculously ornate silver tray she only used for appearances, she knew she'd have to get to the point quickly if she wanted to get out with her pride.

"When did it start?" he asked.

"A matter of months, but I let it go too long."

"And now you're afraid."

"It's the doctors. You know how I feel about doctors."

"I know the whole, terrible story. You do know that something's really wrong with you, don't you? It's serious."

"I needed a second opinion. The first one came from a twenty year-old moron."

"I thought you called me down here because you were finally having an affair worth feeling guilty about. And then I get here, and your hair is falling out."

"My hair?"

She turned at the waist to see herself reflected in the television and ran her fingers through her hair. It was thin. None came out in her hands, but she could feel that it had lost its density. "Oh, God," she said. "What am I going to do now?"

"Float out on the cape in your little boat and die, I suppose."

It was too much and he must have known it because he left for the kitchen and came back with a bottle of Polish vodka. She always kept one in the freezer for company, though she rarely drank herself. He poured a shot into her hand-carved driftwood cup, which now seemed unbearably ridiculous to her, and held it beneath her chin.

"I don't want that," she said. "I can't drink in my condition."

"Drink up or I'm leaving."

"Fine," she said. She sipped on the vodka. "But if something goes wrong it'll be your fault."

He took her cup and poured her another. "What could go wrong?" he asked.

She held the cold liquor at the back of her mouth before letting it move down her throat. You couldn't pretend to be pregnant and happy while you were drinking shots. At least she couldn't. Because that wasn't the kind of mother she'd want to pretend to be. She'd want to pretend to be the kind that reads all the books and does all the right things. She'd want to pretend to be the know-it-all in Lamaze class, who shunned the idea of a partner.

"You're such an asshole," she said.

He shook her knee in response.

If they were younger, if they were in better health, if they were still the overly ambitious people they'd once been, or if they were just slightly more vicious in their anger with the world and its dirty damp habit of disappointing, they may have taken down the entire bottle together in a laugh. They may have broken her terrible driftwood art into bits of sticks, hurled it into the cape, and then laugh-cried each other wet in the wheat-colored grass. As it was, he coached her through half the bottle, indulging in what he called second-hand binge drinking, and then they wound up in her bed, looking into the black glass of each other's eyes in the dark.

"What if this was our child?" she asked, stroking her belly.

"Then we'd love it," he said. "I love all of my children."

"But this child would be different. It would be special. It would be the first child born in quite this way. We'd have to whisk it off to a secluded forest refuge and hide it away from the doctors and scientists. They'd want to run tests and stick it with needles. They'd have tubes and wires running in and out of it."

"You're right," he said. He propped himself on an elbow. "I know just the place. My family's cabin in the Hocking Hills. We'll go there without a word, tell no one of our plans. Disappear. And then we'll raise the baby together in the woods. We'll live off berries and roots. Or maybe I'll learn to hunt. I could learn how to kill things."

She sat bolt upright. "Books!" she shouted. "We have to remember to bring books. Otherwise, how is it going to learn?"

He eased her back down into the sheets. "You're in charge of the books. I'll take care of supplies."

She was excited, exhilarated. Happier than she'd been in a long time, maybe happier than she'd ever been. In her jubilation, she risked kissing Warren on the mouth and calling him her husband.

"My wife?" he asked in response.

The last time they were together, it was a post-divorce experiment in the kind of tastelessness that was going around at the time and had resulted in considerable awkwardness—at least on her part. For Warren, the natural conclusion of any interaction was physical intimacy. He slept with mail carriers and baristas with as little contemplation as one brings to opening letters or sipping coffee. Now, they made love as people make love in war. It was an instinctual act with the force of inevitability behind it—*things must go on, even in times like these*—and very little thinking in front of it. It wasn't about pleasure or even pain, so much as it was about relief. When it was over, they fell immediately into their own private realms of rest. In hers, she thought about air moving in and out of her body, she thought about breathing and breath. She couldn't guess what Warren might be thinking, but if it had to do with the fact that he was her ex-husband and she was a lesbian and they'd just made love like a commercial for married heterosexual bliss, she didn't want to think about it.

There was a realization coming, a sense to be made, but she couldn't quite discern the pieces, much less put them together. She found her hands moving absently to her belly, the habit she'd coddled as a sign of her inherent maternal charms, but instead of stroking the bulge, she probed. She pushed and questioned. The thing inside of her made no response to her investigations. It sat like a meaty stone, immobile, immutable. She understood for the first time that it lacked life—it wasn't dead, but it wasn't alive—and this understanding spread like a ray of searing pain through her body.

She woke Warren with a groan and said, "I'm not pregnant with your magical love child."

He looked her full in the face and told her he knew too; he'd always known. Could they please have some breakfast now? She rolled her face into the mattress.

"Then I'll cook," he said. "I'm a better cook anyhow."

She reached over the side of the bed to find a blanket, a bit of clothing, anything to cover her body. Noticing her scramble, he threw a sheet over her head and left the room. Beneath her canopy of cotton, she felt her body's awareness of the facts of the sex they'd had. The smell and the feel of her skin, the brine she knew was his and the brine she knew was hers. They hadn't used protection, whatever that was for anyone. It was what she knew she'd be thinking about if she were a different person in a different life, who'd just done the same thing she'd done with a different man in a different life, but she wasn't a different person in a different life. She was herself.

Warren's cooking was loud and the yell of the yolks hitting the pan slid her out of bed and onto all fours like the human animal she knew herself to be. When she stood, blood rushed in her head and doubled her over. She staggered to find a nightgown she'd taken to wearing in recent months. She never would have worn it in front of anyone as it was nothing but a sack, but she was feeling utterly defeated. She opened all of the windows and the doors to the cape and stood in the wind. She felt the bowling ball at her waist, recalled its desire to sink her to the floor of the lake.

When she came into the kitchen, she was ready for almost anything. Warren had somehow put together a fine spread out of the nothing she'd been keeping in her pantry since she'd stopped eating regularly. "I haven't been shopping," she said. "Normally, I would have."

"There's plenty," he said. "Just sit and eat."

She dipped a corner of dark wheat bread into a yolk and found that she could eat it without great struggle. She was relaxed enough to let it go down without analyzing it. He'd mixed nuts and dried berries and flax seed and she spooned them down with soymilk. He seemed pleased to see her eat.

"It's not so phenomenal," she said. "I've done it all my life."

"Fair enough. Now what in the hell's going on here?"

"I've gone off the deep end. Leave it at that."

He shrugged and went back to the work on his plate. Their conversation rolled around the weather on the cape, the work he was doing on canvas now that he'd forsaken video as thin medium, not substantial enough to support his more serious work. They talked about his kids and the strange consistencies in their personalities, despite their different mothers: they all hated art. "I thought at least one of them would want to pick up a brush, but they're all into sports. Their heroes are athletes suffering from crappy hip-hop," he said.

"Give them time," she said. "They're only toddlers."

"The oldest is twelve now."

"Jesus," she said. "When did that happen?"

"I know. It's like I'm old."

The wind drew the long kitchen curtains up and into the room in a way that she never would have allowed without company, without a day like this one in the room. The fabric could dip into anything, knock any number of jars or glasses from shelves and she almost hoped that it would so that they'd have something to scurry around about, shuffling into a pile to leave for later.

"Listen," he said, suddenly quite stoic. "I'd like to be the kind of man who stays and ferries you through whatever mess you've gotten yourself into here, but we both know that I'm the kind of man who drops everything to visit you and hopes that's enough."

She dropped her toast. It was not that she'd expected—or even hoped—for him to stay with her; rather, she wasn't quite ready to face aloneness, to face herself. "You're leaving?" she said. "Now?" She gestured to the half-empty bottle of vodka on the floor, her billowing nightgown.

"You're already deciding to hate me. I can see it in your face."

"No, I don't hate you."

She'd eaten as though there was nothing wrong, but now she couldn't deny the sickness. She threw up on the floor and black stars spun around her eyes. Once she had her balance back, she started to clean up the mess with her cloth napkin, but then she decided she'd rather watch him clean. "Can you get this for me please? I'm too tired and my head hurts because you got me drunk and fucked me," she said.

He cleaned with the skill of a distracted teen, dropping forks and knives and forgetting them on the floor, and as he did so, he told her that he knew he should do the right thing. He should stay with her and help her get well. He knew that. He knew he should stay with her for however long it took. Years. If necessary, his best years. She'd given him some of hers, after all. But he wasn't going to do the right thing because he was incapable of caring for someone in that way. She called him an asshole, a giant asshole, and told him to get out of her head and her house, but she didn't mean it. It was just the easiest way out of the conversation. "I'll call you," she said, finally. It was a gift she was giving him. He nodded, gathered his things, and then he was gone.

4. *Afterbirth*

Rather than a dream of a do-over life, it was another tumor in her belly. They determined this with long needles and an incision beneath her ribcage. This one had *mass*. It had *character*, but it was ultimately benign. They took it out of her—rather unceremoniously, in her opinion—and declared it to be the largest mass they'd ever removed from the uterus of a living human woman. "How did you manage the pain?" they asked her.

"I didn't feel any pain," she said. "I was happy."

Was she sad now? Not exactly. It wasn't a child she'd lost; rather, it was the idea of a child, an idea she hadn't known she'd needed. When they asked her to submit to a series of tests that might determine how she'd managed to tolerate the intruder for so long and with so little complaint, she told them all to go fuck themselves and so she had her comeuppance. It didn't make her feel any better. In her hospital room, her only company was the bed that bore the name of a girl, Janie, and came equipped with arms that seemed to want to hold her. She slept well in its embrace.

The nurses said she should be up and about by the time the students were returning for the fall semester, but she wouldn't be ready to teach. Recovery would take time. She told them that she had pets and that she read books and drank wine, though this may have been a lie on every count. When she'd gone in for treatment, she'd asked no one to look after her cat, which had gone half-wild in the cape anyhow, and she couldn't imagine reading or drinking.

Rather, she'd taken to thinking of swimming. In real water, open water, the kind of water populated by mystical creatures. The thing about mermaids: the sailors who imagined them weren't inventive enough to give them the faces of women they'd never known. Their mermaids were their lovers and their wives and their mothers, the women who surrounded them in their shore lives. When sailors tattooed mermaids into their chests, they'd always borne the faces of women they'd loved and lost. But Amelia believed she could imagine an entirely new face. One no one had ever seen before, not even her.

THE COLLAPSE

There is no light in the hole. Fifty yards of stratified shale are a drop shade between you and the world. And yet when you wake from the sleep that rises like a fever every four or five hours, you find yourself fooled again by the illusion of light—the mind telling the eye it's an eye. You think if you can hold on long enough it might show you the way, but all it reveals is darkness and darkness beyond that. Nearby, seven men sleep or fail to sleep. After one day in the hole, their names no longer cling to your ideas of them; you know them instead by their voices, the way their bodies smell somehow distinct despite the heavy silt lacquering all of you. You could show the one with the wife-maddening snore what it's like to be jolted out of sleep, but then you'd be denying him his only peace. What kind of man would that make you? You settle instead into the uneven and labored measures of his breathing and let them take you somewhere, anywhere else.

In the darkness, your mind becomes preoccupied with questions your eyes would never allow you to consider in the light. Do your wife and children know your true face as you sense it in the dark? What's the likelihood that you'll be recalled as a man who conducted himself honorably in the end? Would anyone claim you a worthwhile presence? You calm yourself with the novelty of an insect trolling your skin, make a private hobby of the slick of condensation pooling on the stone behind your head. Your fingertip tells you when there's enough to catch a drink of stony, sulfuric water.

You know there are men coming for you. Those who were still on the surface during the blasts, those the company will send, and those the government will by now have dispatched to your gray part of the state. Technicians, all of them. All of them with plans and ideas. They will most likely try to communicate with you by rapping or pounding out patterns. You don't know Morse code well enough to execute it, but when your hands come upon an elbow of pipe in the debris, you declare that you can use it to send messages. *Tell them we're here*, the men say. *Tell them to hurry*.

Time passes, and, hearing nothing from above, you spend hours developing words in this pipe-rock language, a vocabulary broad enough to communicate the broken legs on the lead man, the water that may carry you through another day but no more, the heavy scent of fuel somewhere nearby. And then you laugh, realizing that your language is already dead. How do you expect to teach it to the men on the outside? How will they come to understand your pain, the pressure in your ears, and the thirst that rises in your throat like a burr?

You ask the men if they would mind granting you a reprieve from your duties for an hour, and they don't even suggest passing the pipe to someone else, perhaps sensing that you are unwilling to relinquish your task. Perhaps they understand, as you now do, that there is nothing so vital as a purpose. There are four men guarding the water rations and you wouldn't dream of asking them if the job couldn't be better done by two.

The man you remember from the surface as too thin for this kind of work makes his first pronouncement of the ordeal as a conversation about the allure of tobacco tapers off. *If we don't hear from them soon, they'll never find us.* The others curse at him. You toss a fist-sized rock in the direction of his wavering voice. *We've got a day before we run out of air and water*, he says. *It'll take at least a day for them to dig this deep and if they go too fast, they'll crush us. Either way you cut it, it doesn't look good.*

No one believes him. *Your math is wrong*, they say. They rattle off facts and figures and remind him of ventilation shafts. *Did you factor that into your death wish?* they ask him. He retreats into his silence as the others find reasons to dismiss his claims. His slight frame and weak voice are cited as evidence of his unreliability. He's like a depressive child who only looks at things the sad way. The lead man with the broken legs says in a groaning voice that he's been in worse collapses before. *This is nothing compared to the last one*, he says. *We'll be out of here in ten hours. You watch.*

But like a cancer the thin man's words begin to consume the fragile tissue of hope. You can feel it happening in yourself and in the men around you. For the first time, you allow yourself to experience the full weight of the idea that you may be sitting in your own grave. You picture your four-year-old daughter placing red, white, and blue carnations around the head of the hole you went down. You loved your country. That's something they'll say about you in your obituary. Or perhaps they'll say that you loved your mother.

Soon, efforts to find a loose piling of debris are redoubled. You renew your percussive song with the pipe. *We are here*, you sign, *you must hurry*. You tell the men you're sure they can hear you. You're committed to tapping for as long as your arms can move.

Because you're all very civilized, you pick the deepest region of the hole as the makeshift lavatory. It's far enough away from the area where the eight of you huddle to offer a sense of privacy, though not far enough away to eliminate stench or sound. Your mind connects a man's voice with the yellow Viper he parks next to your broken sedan as he declares he's ready for his third shit of the day. *According to my bowels, which are highly reliable*, he says, *we've been down here for twenty hours.* You ask him if that means he's always grunting on the can like an animal at dawn and he ignores you. *You're the one with the Viper*, you say. He ignores you again.

He then proposes you all take bets on how many hours have passed. Time becomes a matter of intense contention. One man claims he knows it's morning because he's craving eggs. *I always want eggs at exactly five a.m.*, he says. You think of your wife's eggs, the perfect roundness of the yolks in the pan-crisped whites. Your wife no longer prepares your breakfast now that the local rags have sided with the strikers. She says she doesn't want a scab for a husband and leaves your paychecks on the kitchen table uncashed. You've told her that your job doesn't hurt the strikers. It's an office job, and no one would begrudge you for working it. But the truth is that you head down the hole like everyone else. She'll be confused when your name is among those listed as missing. *He's not supposed to be down there*, she'll say. *He works filing papers, for Christ's sake.*

Almost all of you have wristwatches, though none of you can see them. You'd have more equipment if things had gone as they were supposed to go, or if anyone had

paid attention during the training. When the first blast
hit, the crew should have been standing on the surface,
calibrating instruments. Instead, it was packed on a
processing elevator, rushing down to punch the clock.
When the elevator bucked and two men fell into the
shaft, the rest should have ascended. Instead, you all
went down a hundred more feet to rescue them. As the
second explosion tipped you into the nothing from
which you woke with a spinning light in your head, you
were briefly relieved of coherent regret, but now
everything is tainted with remorse. If only you carried a
lighter, if only you chose thicker clothing to wear, if only
you followed your instincts. It isn't right to work
underground.

The thin man speaks again and says he's been
counting. *At least thirty hours have passed*, he says. The
lead man is dubious. *You've been counting this whole
time?* he says. The thin man explains that he was taught
to do this at an operation in northern Kentucky. *If
you're trapped, the first thing you want to do is start
counting*, he says. Someone, probably the old-timer, who
has been working in mines since he was twelve, asks the
thin man why he didn't say something before. *Why'd
you let us sit here all this time jawing about it if you
already knew?* he asks. The thin man responds with a
shade of anger in his voice. *It's hard to count while
you're talking*, he says.

There is a silence and then the other men decide that
the thin man is untrustworthy again for all of the same
reasons that they dismissed his earlier estimations.
Believe me or don't believe me, he says. *I'm going to be
here counting either way*. Your mind wanders and then
you find that you too are counting. Perhaps everyone is
counting. Your tapping on the stone becomes a way of

tracking time. You ease into the repetition and find respite there. It's like a dance you're doing with the rock.

The lead man with the broken legs groans. He apologizes for his groaning. He says he knows it isn't very professional of him, but he can't seem to control it as it happens when he's falling asleep, and he can't seem to stop himself from falling asleep. *It's like a spell*, he says. The old-timer warns that if the lead man falls into a deep sleep, he's unlikely to wake up. *He'll be dead before they get to us*, he says. The men agree to take shifts, tapping the lead man's shoulder if he groans. He thanks them every time.

The idea of losing the lead man is hard to get your head around. It was he who'd assembled the crew, a pack of men who hardly knew each other from lives that rarely overlapped; he who'd said you were destined for bigger things in Sugar Creek; he who'd always seemed to know instinctively how to get a man to do his best under less than ideal circumstances. You were passing a lazy afternoon with your family when his call came. *Come on*, he said. *You aren't the type to sit on your ass when there's money to be made, are you?*

Your wife called you a bastard for going back to the mine when there were honest families starving on strike. *See if I'm here when you get back*, she said. *Just try me.* You told her you were demonstrating true loyalty as you walked out, the kind a real man shows by supporting his family in hard times. *Watch and see if you learn something*, you said. If you die down in this hole, the lesson she will learn is not the one you meant to teach her. She will live the rest of her life knowing how right she is and how terrible it is to be right.

It was the lead man's idea to follow the men who'd fallen down the shaft. Like a soldier, you'd followed his commands without question. Now you wonder what will happen if he dies. What will you do? Listen to the old man? Obey the chattering teenager? *Tell us about the kind of equipment they'll use to get down here*, you say to no one in particular. You toss your sound into the room. The man with the snore says they'll come down with a drill and make a hole the size of a man's arm first. If they find anything, they'll make a bigger hole with a larger drill. *What if they don't find anything?* you ask. He tells you they'll keep making small holes until they do. Then the yellow Viper, coarse in every way possible, says that he can handle being trapped, but he doesn't think he can handle being in a hole with a dead man. You tell him you'll kill him before it comes to that. And the first fight breaks out. Men lunging at men in the dark. Somehow, no one touches you. No one even comes near you. You begin to wonder if you exist in bodily form. Perhaps you have shifted into a gaseous state. You cannot disprove this theory unless you touch a man, but you are unable to force yourself to do so.

The second fight happens when the thin man says he's ready to die. He has accepted his fate, he says. They all seem to go after him at once. He screams out in pain and then his screams are muffled. They subdue him and force him to a higher area where the debris is more fragmented and uneven. *I'll just stay here and count*, he says. *You don't have to worry about me.* Again, you are left untouched in the scuffle. You hold your hand in front of your face and are as unsure of its presence as you are of God's presence in the air.

Your efforts with the pipe renewed, you're dutifully tapping away on the rock, making your words with patterns and beats, when you first think you hear a sound. There's nothing, only the sound of the men breathing, and so you start tapping again. The second time you hear the sound, you're sure of it. *Listen*, you say, *do you hear it? It's a voice.* You hear them upright themselves in the dirt, their legs scraping in debris. All is silent and then you hear it again. *Hello*, it says. *Do you hear me?* Your head is tilted to the rock ceiling, but you already know the sound is coming from below.

It's one of the ones who fell off the elevator, says the thin man. *I had a feeling he was alive.* This time, no one disagrees with him, though the impulse flutters in your chest. You want to tell him that you wish he was never born, much less stuck in a hole with you, but you can't endure another fight, so all you say is that he must have heard your tapping and come toward it. You ask the lead man what you should do. You use his name for the first time since the explosions. *Gambut*, you say. *Should we try to dig to him, or do we need to conserve energy?*

A man tells you that Gambut is gone. *Gone to sleep?* you say. *Gone*, he says. You wonder how long the others have known this. Surely the two sitting next to him have known for as long as he's been dead. But they wouldn't want to say because of what the yellow Viper had said. And perhaps because they were afraid of not knowing what to do. *All right*, you say. *We've got to yell to him, see if he can hear us.* You make a plan. You'll all say the word *hello* at once. Then you'll say *seven trapped*. Then you'll say *one man down*.

The voice yells back, *Water?* Without consulting, you all say, *No*. None of you want to share with this man who is, in some way, responsible for your presence in the hole. If he and his friend hadn't fallen, you wouldn't have followed. Then he says, *Rescue soon?* And, without consulting, you all say, *No*. You don't know when it came to this, but you've all taken on a negative outlook. Gambut's disappearance in the dark is surely a factor.

There has been no sign, no sound from above. The thin one says another day has passed and more. He says, *We're all going crazy because there's no clean air.*

A voice near you says that he thinks he can see your eyes when he hears you turn your head, but he knows that can't be right. *My mind is playing tricks,* he says. You think about it. *Maybe,* you say. *Can anyone else see my eyes?* No one says a word, but you can hear some of them nodding. Then you realize you can't hear nods. You don't have that kind of power. *I'm going to keep them closed now,* you say. *And I'm going to keep tapping.*

The voice is gone for a long time, disheartened perhaps by your negative attitudes regarding rescue. And then it's back again with what sounds like a bargain. *Do you have water? I know the way to a lower shaft,* it says. The old-timer laughs. *We might be scabs, but we're not fools,* he says. Others laugh too. You find yourself laughing. Like a child desperate for acceptance, you say, *How stupid does he think we are? A lower shaft?* And yet you already believe in your core that the trade is well worth it: a drink of water for a chance of escape. Later, you risk floating the idea of a vote. *Why don't we decide this democratically?* you say.

The men argue about how to vote anonymously and fairly in the dark. Piles of rocks, yeas and nays. The yellow Viper puts an end to all of that. *Let's say we dig through and find him,* he says. *Which one of you wants to give up his water so he can have a drink?* No one answers and so the matter is quietly settled. You're all too greedy to take a chance on an outsider. In a way, it's a relief. With the burden of indecision and moral pressure lifted, you can now go back to your habit, the reassuring twang of pipe on rock. On the other hand, it probably shouldn't be so easy to make this kind of decision. *What would Gambut tell us to do?* you ask. The yellow Viper tells you he's trying to be polite about this, but he's going to have to ask you to drop it. *It's a devil's bargain*, he says. *Let it go.*

The thin man breaks his long silence, emerging from his isolated perch above to laugh at you. Then he's so angry he's screaming. *Jesus, didn't any of you study the plans?* His voice blades the air. *The lower shaft goes down, not up.* There's no hope of contradicting him. You didn't study the plans. Worse, you weren't aware of the existence of the plans. The most you have learned of the geography of the mines in your months of working them is where to punch your card and where to eat your lunch.

The others are now resolved in their sense that the voice is only trying to steal from them. *I've met ones like him*, says the old-timer. *They'll hold you under to keep their heads above the water.* Without your help, they invent an edict: anyone who tries to help the man is on his own. Plus, he forfeits his rations to the others. When they move to the center of the huddle to shake on it, you silently recuse yourself out of pride, but it's possible no one notices your absence. They wouldn't know you by your face, much less the shape or feel of your hand.

Soon, a new loneliness arrives. It lodges in your head like a song. Your taps on the rock are your only way of saying you regret almost everything you've done in your life, and you've foolishly written them in a language no one else can understand. When you head to the nether regions of the hole to relieve yourself, forcing your pipe ahead of your walk, the voice is there, but you're not interested in talking to it now. You're tired of picking sides. *Leave me alone*, you say. It tells you the lower shaft leads to a system of corollary elevators. *Tell the others I know we can make it*, it says.

You know what sleep has done to Gambut, and yet you can't resist it when it comes. It warms like a blush in your neck and face. Soon you're in a dream you know is a dream because your wife is in it and she's telling you she's pregnant again. This has happened already; it's a scene from your life. *You can't be pregnant,* you say. *We can't afford it.* She plays with the strip of lace cuffing her sleeve. It's the same lace she has used on the edging of all your pillowcases. Cheap, off-white. *Do you want me to throw your baby away?* she says. *Is that what you're asking me to do?* You tell her you're not asking her to do anything; you're just telling her what she already knows. *There isn't room here for another baby.*

When you wake, you already know what you're going to do, but you have a hard time admitting it to yourself. It's easy enough to gather your things—all you have is your pipe—but striking out on your own isn't your style. It goes against your grain. You make the excuse of needing to piss again and no one bothers you as you climb into the hole, but then they want to know what you're doing down there when they start hearing your pipe banging and scraping away. *What's going on?* they yell.

The scent of human excrement is overpowering but once you make your way through the first layers of seepage and debris, a doubly rank chemical presence scrapes the inside of your chest and head. Its wet is on everything, slicking dirt into mud. On your hands and knees, you dig with your pipe, testing for weak areas and then pushing through with your body. You know someone will come to confront you eventually and you're prepared. You've worked out what you're going to say. *Let's talk about this like reasonable human beings.* The yellow Viper surprises you by using those kinds of words on you. *Let's be reasonable about this.*

Your first swing with the pipe is lucky. It's a startled, defensive impulse. Your second swing is about proving a point. You test where he is with your feet and then nail him. The third swing is about silence. *Does anyone else want to try me?* it says. You drop your pipe and resume your harried dig with your hands. You're pretty sure you're dead, but then your awareness of yourself confirms otherwise. Leaking fuel has scarred your insides. Your eyes are wrapped in the stinging gauze of it. In order to move away from the chemicals in the air, you must build a barrier between yourself and it. You stack rocks behind your body as you remove them. The voice tells you you're close, but you've got to work quickly. *The fuel is too much,* it says. *It'll knock you out if you're not careful.*

You remember this man from the surface as a scientific official of some sort. He was holding an instrument in the air when the elevator threw him. The other man who went down the shaft with him may have lost his head as he banged down the hole. You thought you saw that happen, blood misting around his neck, but can't be sure. You're afraid of coming upon his loose head as you dig. What if it asks you why you hit the yellow Viper so many times? What if it holds you accountable for all your sins?

The light, when you reach it, is a silt-heavy revelation, a particulate sludge hanging in the air. You know the taste of it in the back of your throat. The wet on your hands is blood. You've torn your skin to tatters, digging in the rock. If the others follow the scent of your blood, they'll be able to find you. You take off your shoes and fit your socks over your hands, killing the trail. It's possible you could stand in the half-destroyed passageway, but you are by now used to your limping crawl. You imagine yourself a three-headed dog, patrolling your territory.

When you find the voice, it doesn't belong to the man you expected. *I saw your head explode on the wall,* you say from the ground. *It was a pink detonation.* He drags you by one arm and one leg to a level platform, the swaying gaslights tilting the walls. *Now, stand up,* he says. You tell him you can't stand. *I don't have hands,* you say. He says he knows you can stand. *If you can dig, you can stand and if you can stand, you can walk.* You say, *No. No, no, no, no, no. You don't understand.* He tells you he's not carrying you. He pushes the bald steel toe of his boot into your side. *Get up,* he says.

At this point, you're beginning to see you're on different pages. You can understand his perspective, but his insistence strikes you as unfair. What does he know of what you've endured? Your soul is pulverized grit. He leans into your face. *What of the others?* he asks. *Are they dead?* Now he's touching a nerve. You tell him Gambut is dead. *He's dead!* you shout. *Do you know what that means?* The man sighs and straightens himself. *It means there's at least one man down. What of the others?*

You don't want to talk about the others. *Forget about them,* you say. *Just forget about it.* He's not deterred. You can see it in his neck, the hard swallowing he's doing. *Look, there's nothing more to say about it,* you say. *They're in there and we're out here. That's all.* He seems huge and you know he must be bigger than you, but the way he stands over you—it's like he's a different species. *They're all dead?* he says. You pound your sock-covered fists in the dirt. *Of course they're all dead!*

I can't tell what's wrong with you, he says. *You might be insane or you might be an evil bastard.* Because you desire to answer honestly, you think about it. Your wife has lodged similar complaints about you in the past. More than once, you have wanted to expose the inside of your thoughts to the inside of her thoughts. See if she can make sense of the language of your grief. *I'm not an evil bastard*, you say. *But I might be a crazy son of a bitch.*

He laughs and you know you've passed his test. *Let's walk*, he says. *There's work to be done if we're going to live.* And just like that you have your legs back. They carry you away from the roiling calamity in which you were trapped. *Got any food or water?* he asks. *Of course*, you say. *There's a motherfucking three-course meal waiting for you upstairs.* You both use your hands to move rock away from the path that will lead you to the other system of elevators. And then you use your legs and your feet. And then you use your entire bodies to pry.

The top is brighter than you remember as possible. It seems to want to burn itself into your retinas. When they ask you about the others, you're expecting it. You've prepared a statement. *They were too weak*, you say. *It was up to the strong to deliver their message.* You begin extemporizing about how they wanted their wives and families to know that they died bravely when you realize they might still be rescued alive. And how will you explain what happened? You settle for saying that Gambut was very brave. *He was a leader among men*, you say. You weep into the red foam of a microphone and apologize. *I think something's wrong with my head.*

They need your help finding the others. You'd really rather be heading home. You think it would be best for everyone if you just went away. But, for the sake of appearances, you point to areas on diagrams you've never seen, not knowing for sure if your gestures are consistent. You ham your shredded fingers on the paper and hope for the best. When they come back with a plan to follow your tracks, you realize the others will surely survive now. *Do you know how much fuel has leaked down there?* you ask. *One spark and the entire city is a hundred feet in the air.*

They don't listen to you. *You're making the same mistake we did,* you tell them. But they're brave and careless. When they emerge with Gambut's broken body strapped to a desk chair, you throw your hands in the air. *Thank the Lord,* you say. *Thank the Lord!* Family members stream through the barricades, and you wait for your wife and children to surround you with their bodies. You wait for the warmth of your little girl against your side. When they don't show, you suspect it's because they already know you've behaved shamefully. They've watched the entire show inside your head. You refuse medical attention and walk home.

The dresser drawers are hung out like mouths, expelled clothing on the floor. Your mattress is stripped, and there's a note pinned in the middle. Your wife says you're dead to her. It's already morning when you realize she doesn't know. She's left you in advance of your tragedy and hasn't had time to get back and retract. You sit on the porch and wait. Who leaves a man who just got exploded down a hole? The leaves scuttling the woods tell you of every step your family is making back to you. In a dream, your wife's legs open and engulf you. Inside of her, you look out her eyes and see a yellow Viper approaching your drive. The man inside carries an ax with him and it takes you apart without even touching your skin.

When you wake, he really is there. He's sitting on your railing, his face clean shaven but knotted with black medical thread. *You left us for dead,* he says. You take a long time answering and then you tell him you almost didn't recognize him in the light. *You look different,* you say. He turns his cheek and displays the gash that runs from the corner of his mouth to his ear. *Twenty-seven stitches,* he says. *They all belong to you.* You ask him if he's there to kill you and all he does is laugh. *I wish you'd quit wasting my time,* you say. He drags you by the shirt into the yard and pounds bright explosions into your face.

At the end of it, he asks you why. *I consider you my murderer,* he says. Blood salts your teeth, and your tongue is stabbed and fat in your mouth. You have nothing for him. When he rolls you onto your stomach, you assume he's going to put a shovel into the back of your head. You say to your wife, who you now sense was only waiting for a reason to leave your side and will never return, no matter how many collapses you survive, *I should have married a woman with less pride.*

PEEK-A-BOO

Something about the rusty orange of the scrub brush down by the river draws Martin on winter afternoons. The color is nice against a blue or gray sky. He often considers painting a stack of bald tires and other scattered debris near an embankment, though he recognizes the subject matter as less than compelling—a painting that has failed in advance of its creation. The mess becomes his destination nonetheless as he strolls, cigarette burning in hand, to observe the clotted surge of half-frozen water as it passes the scene. He can usually expect to be interrupted only by the occasional startle of a bird or small animal, but today a teenaged girl leans into the gutted maw of a trashed washing machine. Her red skirt is a triangle above two columns of meaty thigh, white flesh exposed through tears—the intentional kind—in her black tights.

"Excuse me," he says. "I didn't know anyone was here."

She pulls herself out of the machine, revealing a top half ribbed with safety pins and interlocking chains. Her hair is a mass of dyed-black tease and silver studs anchor her heavily lipsticked mouth. He knows this look. Many of the female art students he teaches at the university have adopted a kind of threatening dishevelment, an appliqué of the gutter. This girl looks legitimately dirty. "You here for sex?" she asks. She couldn't be more than fifteen years old. "I don't do no weird."

"I'm Martin," he says, inexplicably. Adding, "I'm a teacher," as a kind of assurance, perhaps a deterrent. He doesn't want to be mistaken for a John.

"Really? You don't look like a teacher," she says, surveilling his paint-splattered slacks, the tears above both knees.

His studio is only a few hundred yards away. He could be there in minutes, on the phone with child services or whatever agency handles these sorts of things. Teenage prostitutes, runaways. Instead, he drops his cigarette, pulls his pad from his bag, and begins sketching her in charcoal. She takes to the idea quickly and poses for him. At first she's merely smiling and preening, but then she vamps it up. She grips her knees, hips cocked to the side. She shakes her rear. He risks asking her if she wouldn't mind slowing down a little, so that he has time to capture each pose with a full sketch.

"I'm not as fast as a camera," he says, "but I can usually get a good model down in five or six minutes."

"Now you're an artist," she says.

"That's right," he says. "I'm an art teacher."

"And I'm a *model*," she says. With little talk between them, they manage to establish a routine: he signals to her that he's finished with his sketch by flipping the page on his pad and she invents a new pose. He flips a page, and she lifts her small breasts, which he renders on paper as pert, adolescent bulbs. He flips a page, and she sucks sloppily on a lone finger, which becomes a wrist-smudged thrust.

"Hey, art teacher," she says. "You ever fool around with your students?"

Pinioned, he drops his charcoal. He no longer makes a habit of misbehaving, but on occasion he may risk his career by sleeping with someone he shouldn't—one of his own students, perhaps, or one of his colleagues' students. On the whole, his romantic choices are bald matters of convenience. He's there, she's there; it happens, it ends. In the twilight of his life and career, he has learned to lower his expectations. He has not yet endeavored to discover how low they can go.

"Do I look like I'd do that sort of thing?" he asks.

She studies him, her mouth a wry tilt, and he feels his organs clench under the pressure of her gaze.

"We can stop this right now," he says. "I'll put my pad away."

"I was only joking," she says. She smiles, laughs at him. "Pick up your crayon."

There's a kind of comedy to her next series of movements, which are so over-the-top as to peel away from sexuality and become something else. A silly act, a performance. They both laugh a little—he as he fills page after page with quickly rendered, gestural sketches and she as she invents increasingly fantastic poses, all of them infused with the clichés of porn: breasts compressed between fists, tongue darting through V of fingers. It's the most exciting session he's ever had with a live model. He would never dream of asking a professional to do what this girl is doing of her own volition.

When she leans over and flips up her skirt to show him her bottom, he notices grime in her underwear, a grassy discoloration between her legs, and considers stopping her again. Has she been down in the dirt with someone? She pulls the panel of stained fabric aside and pulses a finger inside herself, holds the pose. He meets the eyes in the head hanging upside down between the cold-pinked thighs and has seen enough. He snaps his pad shut and tucks it into his bag.

"I'm going to get you some help," he says. "Wait here."

The spell broken, she pulls down her skirt and stands, shakes out her legs and goes back to tinkering with junk. Prodding tires and lifting rusted springs with her combat boots. At the trailhead, he looks over his shoulder to find her holding a tallboy and bringing his discarded cigarette to her lips. For a fleeting moment, he considers inviting her to join him in his studio. After all, she has to be cold without any coat and the nearly bare legs. The decision is made the moment he pictures her spreadeagle on the twin mattress that functions as a makeshift couch in his space. He shouts back to her, "You'll wait here, right?" She nods and sits obediently on a heap of coiled and rusting fencing material, hands folded in her lap.

As he walks, he imagines events as they must unfold. He'll call the operator and say he saw a young girl who might need some help, she'll advise him to speak to the police and connect him directly. And then what will he say? It's unusual for a young girl to loiter by the river, but not illegal. If he mentions the posing to the police, they'll take him for a pervert or a predator. He decides to skip that detail and emphasize the girl's age—she's a child, a little lost girl playing dress up—and ask only that they send a squad car around. Whether or not they hurry about it will be their own concern. He wants this out of his hands.

Things proceed pretty much as he expects with the sole exception that the police ask him if he'd like to file a complaint. Did she proposition him? "She was just— *there*," he says. In a few minutes, he's got a canvas on the easel and he's working, transferring the first of the sketches to the surface in pencil, mapping it out large-scale. Within the hour, he's got the first passes of color down, the big shapes roughed into place. It all comes together cleanly, smoothly. The work is vivid. He forgets to eat. Then, eventually, he's straining to see the painting. It's night and he has neglected to turn on any lights. As he steps back from the work, to take her in from head to toe, he's flooded with the sudden, burgeoning knowledge that he may have left that girl to a dark fate. What if someone less scrupulous has come upon her? What if she's too impaired to resist? What would that mean about him? He returns to the scene and makes a cursory pass of the river embankment, probing the stack of tires and debris with a flashlight, and finds no sign of her. In truth, he does not want to find her.

When he finally comes forward to identify the missing girl on the news as the one he happened to see down by the river, he expects to be forced to explain himself. If he was concerned enough to phone the police in the first place, why did it never occur to him to follow up in some way? No one questions him; he is asked only to offer his version of events, a simple timeline, any helpful details he can muster. He hands over photocopies of the least compromising sketches done on-scene and then opens his Sunday newspaper to find full-scale reproductions of his work juxtaposed with family photographs. The likeness is striking.

When the controversy surrounding the various failures of law enforcement begins to swell—this is not the first lost girl they have ignored, but rather a string of disturbingly similar cases—he expects to be molested by the press. Instead, he's left largely to the margins of the story, the doddering artist who at least tried. There's a reward for information about the girl, who is apparently very troubled. Given the passage of time, her tendency to engage in dangerous behaviors, there's little hope she'll ever be found alive. Martin puts himself on a news embargo. He resolves to forget about the girl and return to the drudgery of his work in the classroom, the subdued Midwestern landscapes that have carried him into obscurity.

He knows it's the girl's father. Who else would it be, standing at that sharp angle, fists balled? The man is costumed in an ill-fitting blazer, a gesture in keeping perhaps with the formality of the occasion, but he's clearly out of place in the gallery with his work boots and voluminous blue jeans. He sidles up to the largest canvas and hips his hands, revealing the cell phone clipped to his belt in the manner of a tool. Martin assumes, then, that he must be a foreman of some kind, a man who bears a measure of authority, but most likely works out-of-doors all day.

The man is at pains to arrive at a suitable positioning for his body as sleek art patrons move around and in front of him to observe the canvas. He's a misshapen boulder in a stream of swift commerce. Martin knows better than to approach him. Why force the confrontation? And yet he can't resist watching as he leans like a reluctant plank to observe at close range the filthy clutch of blooms that Martin has painted into his daughter's exposed crotch. It's the pose that ended the modeling session, the step too far. He wants to spare her father the sight, of course. It's not a pretty painting. But, in a sense, that's the whole point. She's no angel. *You here for sex?*

He wonders if the father knows this side of his daughter. What does any father know? It's the kind of question the paintings deliberately court, but Martin has scarcely allowed himself to consider: what might it be like to witness the girl's actual father meeting her painted gaze? It's one of the reasons he has staged the exhibit as far from Ohio as he can manage, in an exclusive alcove of the Houston art market, which is dominated by oil and pharmaceutical interests. If the paintings sell, and he is assured they will, they'll wind up on the walls of executive suites, never to be seen again by the broader public.

In addition to fearing some kind of retribution from the girl's family, he's all too aware of the moral cowardice spreading through the series like the lace of a toxic mold behind a wall. He was the last one to see the girl and is, by default, the custodian of her last known moments, which he has now chosen to exploit with the sale of graphic paintings that trade largely on the notoriety of her case. He's not sure what that makes him, but he knows he's not a hero. The girl's name was—is?— Katie Parsons, a fact he discovered on the news and subsequently made the title of the series: *Katie Parsons, Missing*. And instead of fifteen, she's nearly eighteen years old, which, according to one colleague, will at least spare him the exasperation of distinguishing the work from child pornography.

Despite the unsettling realization that the man in the awkward jacket is roughly his own age, which reminds him that Katie could be his own daughter, Martin stands his ground when their eyes meet. He then surprises himself by approaching him and inviting him to speak in the courtyard. "Perhaps you'd like to talk in private," he says. The man frowns but allows himself to be led by the elbow outside, where there is a series of marble benches surrounded by ferns in pebbly gravel.

"Would you like to sit?"

"I don't imagine you care very much about what I'd like," he says, erasing any doubt in Martin's mind that he's a family member.

"You're Katie's father?"

"You've seen me on the news."

"No, I'm only guessing," says Martin. He adjusts his collar. "I've tried to stay away from all of the media coverage."

"Let me get straight to the point," says the father. He waves his hands, an expression of irritation, tinged with outrage. "You say you left her sitting on a pile of junk, but only you and she know what really happened."

Martin pulls a copy of the catalog from his interior breast pocket and unfolds it. "I did try to help," he says. He points to the passage in which he describes his meeting with the girl in great detail. The text even includes a transcript of his call to the police—irrefutable evidence of his involvement, of his attempt to do the right thing. The father pulls a pair of drugstore bifocals from his pocket and holds them, still folded, to his face as he reads. Meanwhile, in very plain language, Martin insists that the series is not meant as an assessment of Katie's moral character.

"I painted only what I saw, no judgment," he says. "We all hope Katie will return safe and sound one day soon."

He hears the hollowness of his own words. He knows. Anyone with a brain can see what the paintings say about Katie. *What did she expect would happen, dressed like that?*

"No, no, no. I've heard all of this before," says the father. He shoves the paper into Martin's chest. "I know she solicited you for sex. You don't bother to deny that."

"I'm afraid so," says Martin. "I'm sure it's not an easy thing to hear about your daughter."

"So, when it comes right down to it, it's your word against ours."

"I'm not sure I see your meaning."

Martin is aware, keenly, that he has somehow let the situation spiral out of control. He has rehearsed this scene and others like it, mapped things out entirely in his head. The key is to convey sympathy, but not to the degree that this will invite further involvement or entanglement. *I'm sorry for your loss, let me show you to the door.*

"I'm saying she's owed," says the father.

"I could have done more for her," says Martin. "That's true. I've struggled with that morally."

"How much for the biggest painting, the one where she's bent over like that?"

Flummoxed, Martin shrugs. "I don't know," he says. "I'd have to ask. The gallery arranges these things."

"But you know the range. How much?"

"I think, and I hope I'm not being presumptuous here, that it's probably out of your range. I could offer you one of the sketches at a more reasonable price. I wasn't planning to sell any of them, but I'm sure we could come to an arrangement. These are special circumstances."

"No, I'll be taking the big one. That one right there." He points through the glass at the largest painting, the ten-foot canvas that is the centerpiece of the show.

"It's called 'Peek-a-Boo,'" says Martin.

"Right." The father hands him a slip of paper. "That's the address where my family lives in Ohio. You can have it shipped there. We'll be expecting it."

Martin knows he'll pay up before the glass doors have folded behind Katie Parsons' father. It takes some wrangling. In the end, he has to buy back the painting from the CEO of a wind energy firm who purchased it sight-unseen before the show had even opened. Four-hundred thousand dollars—and that's beyond his cut from the gallery. Probably enough to buy a whole city block in small-town Ohio, he thinks. He ships the painting himself, at his own expense. And he uses the sale of the remaining paintings to remove himself entirely from the university, the town, the state. He doesn't want to see what that money will wring, he doesn't want to be seen.

Shamefully, almost despite himself, Martin watches feverishly for the re-emergence of "Peek-a-Boo" on the art market, convinced it might fetch an even higher price. But if the Parsons are planning to sell, they're biding their time. He wonders if they display the painting in the family home. Where? Above the couch? Do relatives and friends visit it like a vigil, burning candles and re-positioning cheap plastic carnations at its base? Do they allow their eyes to be drawn to the focal point of the painting, the heap of swamp-green contamination between Katie Parsons' legs? No, Martin decides. They must avert their eyes. They must prefer not to see what I have seen.

This is his fear: he's haggling over the bill at a subpar roadside diner and realizes, as he throws a crumpled five at her chest, that the raccoon-eyed waitress is Katie Parsons; he's driving through the night to meet his colleague's new wife and realizes, as she opens the door in a hot pink bathrobe, that she's Katie Parsons; he's fucking his attractive but woefully unskilled new assistant on the couch and realizes mid-thrust that she's Katie Parsons. He cannot stop himself from coming. And then he's the father of Katie Parsons' unwanted child, and the child disappears one day while walking alongside the river, and then he must spend the rest of his life hunting himself down so that he might prevent himself from painting what he's painted. His therapist suggests he *paint through the trauma*, but it's not pain or suffering he must overcome to work again. Like a Catholic, he decides, he must confess.

With the help of an intermediary, he learns that Mrs. Parsons was deceased at the time of Katie's disappearance and that Mr. Parsons has also since passed. He manages to track down Katie Parsons' siblings and chooses the youngest because she's the only girl among the surviving three and he doesn't want to deal with an angry brother. He contacts her by phone, explains he's representing the artist Martin Shuron, and asks if she'd be willing to meet. "He wants to follow up with the family for purely altruistic reasons," he says of himself.

The girl is confused. "Do you have information about Katie?" she says. "I'm not sure, but I think there's still a number for that if you do. We had a reward set up, but that was years ago."

"No, I'm not looking for a reward," he says. "It's about the painting."

He's met with silence, then a sigh. "We don't usually talk about that," she says.

He stammers. "I—I'll understand if it's too painful. I know it's not a very flattering depiction."

"Oh, it's not that," she says. She releases a muted snort. "Though, if you ask my opinion, it's an ugly painting. I know it's supposed to be very valuable, but I think art should put something nice into the world, you know?"

Martin's tongue is a bowtie but she saves him by continuing in a hurried, reeling tone that suggests a certain loneliness. She's the youngest of four children, he realizes, the one to whom no one goes for an opinion. No one has ever bothered to ask this girl about her sister. "People have offered to buy the painting over the years, of course, but my father never wanted to sell," she says. "I think he felt it was, like, the last piece of Katie or something. He didn't want to let it go. But, it's hard to see the point of hanging onto it now. Dad's gone, if Katie hasn't come back by now, what's the likelihood she's ever coming home? And I'm sorry, but nobody in this family is going to tell you we don't need the money. Have you ever been to Athens?"

He manages a grunt in the affirmative.

"There's just one word for it," she says. "Bleak. I wouldn't wish this place on my worst enemy, you know?"

"So, the money could help you make a better life?"

"Florida," she says. "F-L-O-R-I-D-A. My kids like the beach, but their father could take it or leave it. I can't speak for what my brothers would do with their shares. They're into fishing and boats. Maybe they'd do something with that." She pauses, perhaps considering what other options might present themselves to her brothers. "I'm sorry," she says. "Who did you say you were again?"

"We can offer you two hundred thousand for it," he says. "Cash."

When he arrives at the house, he is met not by the youngest of the three siblings, Clare, but rather her brothers, Larry and Dennis, two large, hulking masses. Larry is holding a computer printout of a photo of Martin, so there is no need to pretend. He introduces himself as himself and says he thought it best to come in person after all. "It's been a long time since I've driven through southeastern Ohio," he says.

"Same old, same old," says Dennis. "That about sum it up?"

Martin confirms that Dennis' math is right. Virtually nothing has changed in the five years he's been gone. The college town is still the college town, collapsing porches and pizza joints; the surrounding hills are still the surrounding hills, trailers bleached on exposed outcroppings, dogs yammering on chains. Small-talk exchanged, they agree to get down to business. He is ushered quickly through a living room in which four children—all of them boys with identical buzz cuts—are completely immersed in a video game. They acknowledge him only by leaning around his body as he passes in front of the screen. "Excuse me," he says, needlessly. He is nothing to them.

Clare and the wives of the two brothers are arranged around a table in the kitchen, coffee mugs lifted to their chins. He is introduced to them each in quick succession and is then ferried toward the back door.

"We're going to be talking some business in the garage," Dennis tells the women.

The mention of a garage drives a nervous bolt through Martin's stomach. He does not know what these men may think of him. Perhaps they share their father's opinion—that Martin was a John, or at least no better than a John. Perhaps they believe he bears some responsibility in their sister's disappearance. Perhaps they've been waiting for an opportunity to pound his face, and he's just delivered their fondest wish to them. There's a basketball hoop attached to the garage and a heap of assorted balls and toys beneath it.

"Excuse the mess," says Dennis. "With kids, it's a losing battle. Got any of your own?"

"Nope," says Larry. "According to the internet, he's a lifelong bachelor. A bit of a philanderer." He turns to Martin and shrugs apologetically. "You've got to check up on people these days," he says. "Research. For your own protection, you know?"

Martin does know. His own research, done at considerable expense through a service he located in the phone book, tells him that Larry and Dennis have both seen jail time for minor, alcohol-related offences—public intoxication, driving under the influence. They are not rich men, but they do work full-time jobs in construction-related fields. They are proud members of the NRA, and they have registered as Republicans in the last two elections. Dennis has a degree in meteorology from the technical college, but appears never to have put it to use. Larry quit school in his first year, around the time his sister Katie vanished and was never seen or heard from again.

"Of course," says Martin. "We want to be as open and honest as possible here."

"I'm glad you think so," says Dennis. It's clear, at this point, that he'll be leading the proceedings with Larry running back up or interference. At forty, Dennis is the oldest of the siblings. Perhaps he feels a sense of responsibility, or maybe he's just a take-charge kind of person. He lifts a folder from the top of a grill and opens it. "You quoted a figure to my sister on the phone," he says. "I believe it was in the two-hundred thousand range?"

Martin considers re-inserting an assistant or an underling into the conversation, a buffer between himself and the uncomfortable matter of money but changes his mind when Dennis hands him a sheet of paper. It's a list of the prices his works have taken at auction. It turns out that those in the *Katie Parsons, Missing* series are regularly fetching prices in the one to three hundred thousand dollar range, depending upon the size and condition. Very respectable, though not an accurate reflection of his own finances. He himself has not sold a single painting in three years. He has not painted since his sold-out exhibition in Houston. The original charcoal sketches in his flat files are a constant pressure, a presence. He could sell them and be settled for life, but there would be something untoward about it. Wrong. It would mean something about the kind of man he is.

"I see," he says. "You feel I've lowballed you."

"We just want what the painting's worth," says Dennis. He sweeps his hand in a long, level line. "Not a penny more."

"You have a price in mind?"

Dennis hands Martin another sheet of paper upon which a hand-written figure—$600,000—appears. This means that if Martin purchases the portrait, he will have spent about a million dollars on a painting he has never wished to possess. He's not a millionaire. Far from it. He lives off his limited savings in a combined studio and living space on the south side of Chicago and supplements with cash he earns teaching watercolor painting to retiree hobbyists who don't know who he is. "You understand that circumstances at auction can be very unpredictable," he says. "You never know what might drive up or down the price of a particular piece of artwork."

"I think it's pretty clear that Larry and I are not professionals when it comes to the art world," says Dennis.

"I've never been inside a museum," says Larry. "That's a confession I'll make freely."

"But one thing I do know, and this is because my father told me himself, is that this painting we have here is special," says Dennis. "When Dad came back from Texas, he told us we'd always have an insurance policy hanging on the wall. 'Use only in case of emergency,' he said. We've held off selling a long while. Clare has told you some of the reasons. There are others she doesn't know about too. For one thing, our father didn't want *that*," he points deep into the garage, where the portrait presumably hangs in waiting, "out there representing his daughter. You understand?"

"Of course," says Martin. "It's graphic."

"It's sexual," says Dennis. "It demeans her memory."

"I hope you know I never meant to demean her," says Martin. It's the closest he has ever come to an admission or an apology and yet it isn't entirely true. He pushes himself. "The truth is she terrified me." Thinking of the nonsense about him online, he turns to Larry. "I've never been very good with women."

Larry raises his hands. "Hey, no explanations necessary, man," he says. "To each his own."

"It's just that she, your sister Katie, was very forward. If I'm being honest, I was afraid of what might happen."

"Let's try to stay focused here," says Dennis. "We've given you a price. Can you match it or not?"

"She was a whore," says Larry.

A capillary explosion drains Martin's heart as he stands in place. *Whore.* To hear it said aloud, coming out of the mouth of the brother. Dennis closes his eyes, drops his head. "She was our *sister*," he says, letting a bit of spittle fly into the word.

"She was both. She was our sister and she was a whore," says Larry. And then, suddenly, he's speaking directly to Martin, as though he can expect him to be completely on board with this. "I've never seen any reason to pussyfoot around it, you know? Katie was in and out of trouble her whole life. After she went missing, everybody wanted to pretend like she was someone else. Well, I was there and I knew her. She was who she was."

Martin can see now why Dennis would have preferred to do all of the talking. His brother is a loose cannon. He can't be trusted to remain cool. He'll blow the negotiations. They'll lose their chance to buy their fishing vacations in the Bahamas or whatever it is they've planned. Martin can't bear to haggle with the brothers over price and he can't afford to give them what they want. He attempts to escape the situation by simply leaving and walks around the side of the house to his car. By the time he is seated behind the wheel, the brothers have agreed—in desperation—to lower their asking price to a fraction of the initial offer.

"One hundred thousand," says Larry. "Come on. She's a steal at that price."

Dennis can no longer look him in the eye. "Please," he says. "You can't let us walk back into that house empty-handed. They're counting on us."

Inside the house, the women have prepared a celebratory brunch in expectation of an agreement. They've arranged coffee, orange juice, pastries, eggs, fruit in a buffet on the counter. They tell him to sit, enjoy. "Our house is your house," says Clare. It's an odd thing to say, considering the house isn't hers and it isn't a house where Martin will ever find himself welcome to reach inside a cabinet for a glass. Nonetheless, he appreciates the gesture. He declines the offer of refreshments, but Clare prepares a plate anyway and hands it to him with a paper napkin attached.

"Thank you," he says. "You're very kind."

"It's nothing," she says. She glances at her brothers, who are staged near the sink, drinking coffee in charged silence, and risks slipping in beside him at the table. "I just want you to know, and I hope it's OK that I say so, that you'll be helping this family out a lot with what you're doing. My brothers may be ashamed to say it, but

I'm not. We need all the help we can get." She lifts his hand and places it inside her own, giving it a taut squeeze.

"Cool it, Clare," says Dennis. "Let the man eat in peace."

Martin finds himself searching her face for something of her sister, the lines and shapes he could probably still draw rote from memory, but if it's there, he doesn't see it. Clare is a soft, rounded young woman with an eager smile. He could have seen her at the supermarket checkout and never guessed who she was. He returns her squeeze and smiles.

"I'm very happy to help," he says.

He eats a few grapes and a strawberry out of a sense of obligation. Because he does not now trust either of the brothers to manage the dispursement of funds fairly or evenly, he writes three checks—one for each sibling in the amount of fifty thousand dollars—and hands them out. He sees his mistake the moment it widens Clare's eyes. "And the fourth is for Katie in case she ever comes back," she says. "Two-hundred thousand total, right?"

He writes the fourth check—what else can he do?— and is pulled away from the table and forced into a collective outpouring of emotion. Even the children, the buzzed little boys, are involved. Tears redden their faces and they stomp their feet. The family grasps for each other, they grasp for Martin. He finds himself passed from embrace to crushing embrace. His terror subsides as he begins to believe that he has done right somehow— no matter how wrong it is to give them hope, it's right. As he pulls away in his car, they wave to him from the porch. They continue to wave, he notices, even as he rounds the corner. It seems possible to Martin that they will continue waving to him forever.

Though the Parsons swear up and down that they're packing up the painting right at that very moment and shipping it to the address Martin has provided—a friend's studio with ceilings high enough to properly accommodate the work—the portrait never arrives. This does not surprise him in the least. Nor is he taken aback when he receives notification that the check made out to Katie Parsons in the amount of fifty thousand dollars has been deposited into Dennis Parsons' account. Not even the news that "Peek-a-Boo" has sold at auction for less than a thousand dollars shocks him.

When he rounds a corner in a New York gallery to find himself face-to-face with Katie Parsons again, he doesn't recognize his own work. Then, as her identity dawns, he appreciates the family's ingenuity. Before selling "Peek-a-Boo," they've sliced and flipped the canvas so that only the subject's winking face remains. Her offending bits discarded, Katie is now a disembodied head with strangely buoyant black hair. She's nothing but a pretty girl, unattributed and selling for less than the cost of the supplies once purchased to paint her. He could easily buy the painting, destroy it or hide it away forever, but she's a stranger to him now.

No insult or injury the Parsons can manage to direct toward him or his work will rattle Martin. He considers it all his punishment for succumbing to his own weak need for a kind of forgiveness or comfort he never should have expected them to be able or willing to provide in the first place. He is, however, mystified by Clare's behavior. She writes him frequently, as though dutifully maintaining contact with an estranged uncle. Her flurried and fluid commentary keeps him well appraised of the developments in the Parsons family. What does she want from him? What does she expect?

She tells him about her kids, her certainty that at least one will develop artistic tendencies if she can only manage to expose him to culture. She describes in detail the process of moving to a new home near Toledo. Not Florida, but a decent compromise, in her opinion. She even tells him about her quiet faith, her secret idea that her sister was an angel put on the earth for the sole purpose of showing him, Martin, that anyone can change. *She's your guardian angel*, Clare writes. *She'll watch over you and keep you out of trouble.*

GIRL TRASH NOIR

I knew there was trouble even before I came through the screen door. The blinds were awry, and the child's toys were strewn on the carpet. Leni wasn't the type to leave a room that way. She couldn't tolerate a tilted frame on a wall, much less the view I was taking in as I passed through the living room. Couch cushions tossed, television speared by a baseball bat, a fist-sized hole in the wall. As I stood in the destroyed house, I had the feeling that I was in the process of making a very bad decision, but I made myself walk down the hall.

No one was home. When I saw the cigarettes in the kitchen, a cheap brand and about twenty of them stamped out in a saucepan, I knew the husband had been there. I'd never met him, but I'd heard him described as evil and I knew he made a habit of smoking where Leni told him not to smoke. I called the police from the phone on the kitchen wall and said I thought my friend was hurt, her infant daughter kidnapped. As evidence, I used the handful of hair in Leni's color, vampire red. It was torn out in the bathroom near the sink. There was no blood, but the mattress was shredded to ribbons and stuffing bulged out of all the pillows like guts. The pink dresser drawers in little Alice's room hung empty, and her Cinderella bedding was gone.

The police told me to lock the doors and stay inside until they got there in their cruisers, and I obeyed at first, shutting and locking the front of the house, but then the back of the house was so dark and in such a state of disturbing array. Every last thing was pulled out of the fridge and a full set of steak knives was stabbed into a cooked chicken on the floor. I imagined a man with a serrated blade emerging from the pantry and ran out the back, leaving the door swinging open on its hinges.

Up the hill, McCallister's Gravel was fenced by chain link that was easy to climb. I sat on top of a house-sized mound of white rock. From there I could see Leni's trailer and about three-fourths of her property. If her husband wanted to kill me with a knife, he'd have to invent a way of moving silently over gravel. That, or he'd have to grow wings and land on me. All I could do was wait and watch, which was nowhere near enough to keep my mind from wandering into darker and darker territory. I was already imagining the worst: Leni taking punches to the head, Leni dragged around the house by her hair, Leni left to die in the woods. And then I started seeing the same things happening to me.

It was one of those times I wished I'd never quit smoking, a neutered regret that lead to others. Pretty soon I was wishing I'd stayed in bed that day. Then I was lamenting the day I was born. Why hadn't my mother, a woman with no talent or inclination for mothering, stopped at three? Why didn't someone take her aside and say, "Enough is enough, woman. You've put enough strife into the world." Then I wouldn't be in this mess, watching for a murderer in a half-forgotten trailer park on the edge of nowhere.

I lived with Leni for six months when I was sixteen and trying to stay out of the system. She was a distant cousin and old enough to say she'd serve as legal guardian. I called her out of the phonebook and begged her for a place to stay. She told me, "Sure honey, only I hope you've got some money for things. I sure as hell don't." When we met, she said she was sorry we looked alike on account of the fact that she was so damned ugly. Then she laughed. "I'm only joking," she said. "You're as pretty as a little plum. Meanwhile, they ought to take me out with the trash."

She had a brother who was away somewhere, the army or maybe in jail. And she let me stay in his room, but I wasn't allowed to touch or move anything in there. She wanted it exactly as he left it, down to the camo throw pillows arranged on the bed. We didn't talk much, mainly went about our business, and in six months, I had enough money saved to get a cheap place on my own. Part of the deal was she'd claim I was still living there until I was legal, but only if I stopped in every month for a meal. And then after I was eighteen, I just kept going back to Leni's because it was the closest thing to family I'd ever known.

When she told me she was married it was by way of explaining why my key didn't work in the door. "You don't see him for five years and then he blows right in," she said. "At least this way I'll hear him before he gets inside." She was pregnant even then but didn't know it until later, papers for the restraining order already filed. That's when he started hanging around more. He'd break in, smoke down a whole pack of cigarettes in her kitchen, and leave before she got home. She had him arrested three times. Told me to stay away and so I did. When I finally thought better of it and came back, she had a beautiful blonde baby and an old rifle leaning in an umbrella stand near the door.

All I knew was her husband thought he was the kid's father even if Leni said he wasn't, and he was serving out a sentence that kept getting longer because he couldn't play nice in jail. He once arranged to send a letter inside a children's book instructing the girl to slit her mother's throat and come to him. "He doesn't know a one-year-old can't read yet," she said. "Or maybe he thinks I'm going to read this to my kid aloud." She said jail had soured his mind against all women. And then she said if she ever disappeared I'd know who'd done it. "Rick Merrick," she said. "Remember that name. That's who did it if I'm gone."

The police never did come. It was dark when I left my perch on the rock. I knew I wasn't going back inside that house after nightfall, but I wasn't keen to leave it wide open in back where any stray punk could wander inside and destroy the place and any hope of finding Leni and her girl. I was in the midst of developing a long reach for the knob, my body configured like a relay sprinter's, when I heard a car ease into the drive. I pulled the door shut and went flat beneath the big propane tank in the yard, my head just high enough in the grass and leaves so that I could see the place and not be noticed.

I knew it wasn't the police when they jimmied the lock and walked inside without knocking or speaking. Then the lights went on, and I could see through the crooked blinds that there were two men, both about the same height, both dressed in jackets that could have been military issue or hunting gear. They made quick work of bagging things up and cleaning; they straightened the blinds and moved room to room. Within twenty minutes, they were all through the place. They nearly murdered me with fear, coming out the back with their big black plastic bags, but they only walked through the yard, scanning for debris, and did not take note of me below the tank.

Five minutes later, they were back in their car with the bags and pulling off with the slow ease of the deliberately casual. *Something is up*, I thought. *And it is not good.* I had fifteen minutes to catch the last bus back into the city and a twenty-minute hike to catch it. Every sinew in my body twinged with the urge to bolt. And I knew Leni would tell me to do it. "Get out of here, girl," she'd say. "Forget about me and get on with your own damn life."

But Leni always expected the worst from people. She wasn't friendless, but she kept a low profile on account of the fact that she assumed nobody redeemable would consider her worthy of attention. She was so unused to being addressed politely that kindness of any variety charmed her, which made her an easy mark for predators. I think she half expected me to rob her when I moved in. Not that she ever suggested in any way that she found me suspect or criminal. She was used to being used. How do you give up on a person like that? It would be like punishing an orphan for the fact of her parents' death. *You're alone, so you deserve to be forgotten.* If I walked away, I'd have to decide to hate myself forever. And I guess I wasn't prepared to do that yet.

I knew I could get into the house through a utility hatch beneath the bathroom plumbing, having done it once before when Leni locked herself and her baby out of the house. Going in that way seemed safer somehow, with less risk of being spotted and less broken glass, but it was also terrifying. Like willingly steering into a black hole. I pulled aside the white trim around the base of the trailer and slid through the dark on my back, feeling for the latch, loamy musk of clay all around me. I let myself think of snakes and moved faster. Once inside, I was afraid to turn on any lights, so I slid behind the shower curtains and sat in the tub. I suppose I was waiting, monitoring the scene, holding down the fort. The fact that it might very well be the dumbest thing I'd ever done in my life sat hot like a bullet in my mouth.

Before I found a safe place to stay with Leni, I was more fearless at night. I'd sleep anywhere, but was partial to a moldy squat in the woods, where I'd often fall asleep playing solitaire on my busted-apart sleeping bag. One night the floorboards gave out and I came to with a card on my right eye. I thought I was dead or half-blind. When I realized I wasn't, I put the card—a five of hearts—in my pocket and went right back to sleep. That night in Leni's heavily bleached bathtub told me the extent of my domestication. A cat would jump on the roof or a branch would move on a window, and I'd know her asshole husband was ready to whip back the shower curtains and stab me in the neck. When the curtains finally did part, I'd long come to think of these things as paranoid dreams. Instead, it was a pair of uniformed cops.

They grabbed me by the arms and pulled me out, knocking my head on the toilet on the way though the door. "Who the fuck are you?" they said. "What the fuck are you doing in here?" They never gave me a chance to respond. Out in the yard, the sun like white rock in my eyes, I couldn't see their faces. I threw up my arms, but only shielded every other kick to my head and back. When I finally focused on the thing in front of me, it was a metal toilet in a holding cell. It kept moving on me when I'd try to focus but I managed to catch it and vomit inside. I saw dried blood in my eyelashes and passed out on the floor.

A few days later, I was in a clinic and a male nurse was telling me I'd be fine if I stopped resisting treatment. "I'm not resisting," I said. I tried to say things. My mouth was all water. My teeth were sinking nubs. "What you need is a good dose of common sense," he said. He scrubbed my arms, legs, and chest. "Don't worry," he said. "I'm not trying to cop a feel. I like my ladies with a little meat on their bones." He tapped talcum into my crotch from a pink plastic bottle and stood me up. There was a metal mirror. I looked like a broken tree branch inside it. "Look at you," he said. "Almost pretty." This was my cue to punch him in the balls, but the only revenge I could manage was to vomit. He cleaned me again, roughly this time, dressed me in white scrubs, sat me in a chair, and wheeled me out. "Rotten piece of trash," he said.

For about an hour, I sat in a room with ten or eleven other women, all of them in similar predicaments. Some of them may have been prostitutes, given the amount of makeup still smeared on their faces, but others looked like long-haul truckers, hair buzzed in the front and long in back. Nobody seemed interested in conversation. A television chirped in an upper region. And then a trucker grabbed one of the prostitutes by the hair and shoved her into the floor. Zero provocation. I wheeled myself into a corner and prepared to kick anyone who came near me. I told myself to aim for the teeth and then fell almost immediately into a sleep that felt velvety and eternal.

Then I was sitting in an office that belonged to an official in a suit. A detective? He didn't identify himself and there were no clear signs, no badge or nameplate. He asked me how I was feeling and took his time coming around a desk to take my chin in his hand and wince at my eye. "Nasty," he said. "Wish that hadn't been necessary, but you were out of control. They tell me you tried to bite off an officer's ear."

It was possible. I'd done worse when mortally threatened. But my gut told me he was full of it. "What am I doing here?" I asked him. "Are there charges against me?"

He told me they'd sorted it all out. They knew who I was because they'd found my purse in the tub and matched my name to the one given in the 911 call. He said it was all a mistake, but it was better to err on the side of safety. "What if you were the killer?" he said. "We had to rule out that possibility."

"Leni's dead?" I asked. I thought of her wide face, upturned in a pile of leaves, black lipstick particulate clinging to her lips. "Where did you find her?"

He didn't answer. I could see in his face he wasn't sure what I meant. "My cousin," I said. "Did you find her?"

He turned abruptly and reached into a stack of papers. "That's the thing," he said. "We don't have any record of a person like that." He set a file folder in my lap and dropped into a chair behind the desk. "That's all the research," he said. "You'll even see a transcript of your call in there. But there's no record of anyone named Leni living in that place. And there's no record of the two of you being related."

"We're cousins," I said. I thought of the long, ambiguous line between us. The uncle by marriage whose cousin married Leni's mother when her father died. "A few times removed."

He tapped his shirt pockets and pulled out a pack of cigarettes. I'd have chosen a single Merit over immortal life if he'd offered, but he didn't. He lit up and strolled around his office in a thoughtful way. "All that being said," he said. "We do have a murder to deal with. Low-level pharm mule. Boss has an airtight alibi. What can you tell me about your relationship to McCallister?"

It took me a beat or two to match the name to the gravel pit and the local pill mills. I knew only what everyone knew, which was that McAllister set up shop in the early nineties when moron legislators loosened the laws around pain med prescriptions. He'd been running millions of blues through his so-called clinics since. It was common knowledge he laundered his drug money through property, first buying up foreclosed ramshackles, then grocery and liquor stores, then land. And that's how he came to own pretty much all of Portsmouth, including the lot where Leni's trailer sat and the gravel operation where I'd perched while waiting for the police. So, like a lot of people, I knew McAllister, but I wouldn't know him to see him.

"There's no relationship," I said.

His mouth was a taut red line, cigarette perpendicular. I knew I had to offer some sort of conciliatory information or find myself in a cell again. "I climbed the fence and sat on some rocks there after I made the 911 call, but I'd never been in there before. All I know is, my cousin paid rent to the owner so she could plant her trailer there. She said the guy had her do some work cleaning up the office when she couldn't match the bill. That's it."

"So you admit you broke into the place," he said. "Go ahead and deny it if you want but the security cameras place you there for four straight hours."

"I was waiting for the police," I said. "I didn't expect it would take you a day to get there."

"It was a busy night. Higher priority calls."

The idea that there was a ranking system to violent crimes rankled me. I knew where people like Leni and I fell on most lists, but I'd done a pretty good job up until that point pretending that the world was slightly more just. "If there were cameras, maybe they caught what happened at my cousin's house," I said. "She was gone when I got there, and the place was a mess." He seemed about to shrug, as though to say, *what's so strange about a mess in a trailer home?* I added, "She's got a husband who hits her," and immediately regretted it. Now he had all the parts he needed to float his clichés in the trash parade he was no doubt inventing in his mind.

"The security cameras weren't angled that way," he said. "But they do give us a clear picture of you."

"Then you already know I didn't do Jack but sit on a pile of rocks all night."

"McCallister," he said. He wagged his cigarette at me. "There was a murder, remember? Happened in a utility shed about fifteen yards from where you were sitting. At least thirty rounds dropped. And you want me to believe you had nothing to do with it? With your record, I don't think so."

I thought about it. Wouldn't I have heard something like that? "Unless it happened in complete silence, it didn't happen while I was there," I said. "I was pretty keyed up and scared. I would have noticed any sign of a gunfight."

"We can hold you indefinitely if you're not telling the truth," he said.

The last time I'd been locked up, I was only a child. I spent two months in juvenile detention because I'd taken a swing at a foster mother who made me sleep and eat in a hall closet. And during that time I'd learned how to endure all manner of questions, accusations, indignities. I summoned what I knew of the law. "Believe whatever you want," I said. I let a bit of spittle fly into my speech. "If you can't come up with legit charges within the next ten seconds, you and my lawyer can sort it out. Meanwhile, I'm going to be standing in front of the first camera I can find, showing a reporter my black eye and the teeth falling out of my head."

I let him count out the full ten in silence, maintaining eye contact all the while. It took an effort to stand, but I managed by balancing myself on the desk. "And I'm taking this with me," I said. I waved the folder at him, and he made no move to take it back, so I staggered out the door and down the hall in my prison scrubs and flip-flops. No one tried to stop me, though they all seemed to take me in, pausing in their tasks to gawk. When I made it to the parking lot, the first thing I did was ask a white-haired loony on a bench for a smoke.

"Cigarettes will kill you," he said.

"Do I look like I'm worried about dying?"

He appraised me as he held out his lighter. "You got to learn to take better care of yourself," he said. Then he sang a song for me. *Beat up girl, looks like hell. Beat up girl, she wants to cry. Beat up girl, she's going to die.*

The inside of my apartment looked more depressing than it had the last time I'd seen it. Before, I would have said I was going for a pared-down aesthetic. Streamlined, simple, no fuss. Now it was clear to me that I'd accomplished bland desolation. The place was criminally bleak, not to mention dirty. It made me feel sheepish about the kind of life I'd been living. I made enough money at my computer job to buy nice furniture, but instead I hauled in twelve-dollar thrift store couches and a closeout mattress from Big Lots with a dent in the middle. The curtains on the windows were old bed sheets I'd dressed up with a bit of pathetic fringe at the top. My only pan sat greasy on the stove and I had a sticker in my front window that warned of an attack dog I didn't own. *Warning*, it said. *Pit bull on premises.*

Maybe I'd learned how to live and work in the world, but I'd never let my transient self recede far enough to become a normal kind of girl. Now I wanted scented candles in wall sconces and beaded throw pillows dotting a plush sofa sleeper. I wanted a dozen sophisticated black dresses in my closet, all variations on the same vaguely academic theme. I wanted advanced cutlery in my kitchen and a coffee table topped with Mexican tiles. I knew it was only my brush with death that made me want these things. On a normal day, I would taken great pleasure in leaving on my dirty boots as I flopped into bed. Today I felt so lucky to be alive that I considered undoing the laces before I pried them off my feet.

Here's what I thought I knew: I'd somehow managed to time the previous evening so that I happened to show up to dinner just late enough to miss Rick Merrick raging on my cousin and then climbed into a gravel lot where a notorious pill boss had just made Swiss cheese of an underling. The fact that I walked out the back door of Leni's house just as a pair of goons came in the front door to do a sweep of the property did not escape my accounting, nor did the likelihood that the police who grabbed me out of the tub were members of a task force expecting to find armed thugs in the house. I was lucky they didn't shoot me dead before I'd had a chance to wake up. Then of course there was the ordeal in jail. Anybody could have poked me in the side to get rid of me. Or they could have left me in a cell to rot for weeks, months, or even years. With Leni gone, no one would have come forward to testify to my innocence or ignorance. As far as the police were concerned, she didn't even exist.

I didn't know who would claim my things in the event of my death. I had siblings, but I wasn't sure they'd know me to see me, and both my parents were long gone. The friends I had weren't the kind of friends who'd want to inherit my junk drawer of a life. They were drinking friends—people who recognize you in the bar because you were there the night before. And my job wasn't the kind of job that took much note of no-shows. The data entry business is like a game of musical chairs—the job gets smaller as it gets longer until there's only one desk left in the office. Most people aren't equipped for that kind of stress and irregularity, but I got off on not knowing how long my latest gig would last or how much it would net me.

I was imagining the landlord boxing my things, holding up the items in my limited wardrobe—white tank top, white tank top, white tank top, black jeans— when I realized I might as well have been counting sheep. I was about to fall asleep on my feet. My bed, unmade, the fitted sheet clinging to the mattress on only three sides, was the most beautiful thing I'd ever seen. My dreams were black, lights out, nothingness. My dreams were a mammoth cave or a grave. Then I dreamed Leni was sitting at the foot of my bed, her weight rolling me into her. She was wearing a sugar-colored angora sweater and a green scarf over a shaved head. She had her little girl in her lap and was bouncing her.

"I thought you were dead," I said.

"I am," she said. "But you're making it really hard to rest in peace."

Leni wasn't one for teary shows of emotion, but she let me throw myself in her lap and cry. "It's OK," she said. She patted my head and Alice imitated the motion, setting her little pink hand in my matted hair. "I know you were only there because you care about me. I just wish you'd had the good sense to give up and walk away."

"I knew you'd say that," I said. I wiped my nose in my sleeve and pointed at her. "You never place any value on yourself. It's one of your biggest flaws."

She laughed. "Maybe you're right, but I know I didn't crawl out of the grave just to be insulted by you," she said. "You got anything nice you could say to me? I could use a few kind words about now."

The neon sign on the Chinese place across the street turned the room a red-bottomed ochre. "Leni," I said. "You're mixed up in some dangerous shit."

"Listen, I feel awful about what happened to you. I really do. But I'm here because I need to tell you to back off. What you saw in the house wasn't what you thought you saw, but it was meant to look that way, and I need it to stick with certain people."

"What about the police?"

"What about them?"

"They gave me a file. It says you never existed and we're not related."

She laughed and set Alice on the floor. The girl toddled over to the coffee table and played with a pair of earrings and a bracelet strewn there. "Well, they're at least half right," she said. "If we're related, we'd need a magician to prove it."

"You took me in because you pitied me."

"I took you in because you needed a place to stay."

She lifted Alice and let her play at fitting an earring into her ear. Bands of light shifted the tone in the room to a hollow, fractured blue. "Look, Annie, I know you feel like you owe me something, but you don't. You've got to find a way to let me go and live in peace with the fact that you tried."

"That's something you'd say," I said. "But you're also a mother now and a real mother would want to know that her daughter was going to be OK. She'd want to murder whoever put her kid in danger."

"What do you know about real mothering?" she asked and was gone. Try as I might, I couldn't conjure her again, and I woke sensing that something precious had been stolen from me. At the kitchen counter, I set out all the papers in her file. *No record of anyone residing at that address, no record of anyone responding to that name, no record of any of you miserable people at all.* It only took me a few hours to bait the local PD into downloading a Trojan designed to delete all of their files. I felt no guilt, no remorse whatsoever. If all it takes is a Budweiser bikini and the promise of a peep—*click here to see my huge tits!*—to cripple your operation, you probably deserve to go down.

Three days later, I went back to Leni's trailer and found only a burned out husk with such horrors inside as a melted baby doll speared on a piece of blackened aluminum siding. I knew how they'd done it, exploded the whole thing apart like a firecracker, because the propane tank was still sitting topless in the middle of the heap. The message, such as it was, was clear: full erasure. Maybe it didn't matter who sent it. One of McAllister's heavies, angry cops, Rick Merrick, Leni herself. It was all the same. Though a string of similar messages found their way into the local rag—apparently there was an arsonist targeting meth labs and pill docs in the area—this particular explosion went unremarked upon, unnoticed. Maybe the birds would mourn their feeders blown off the nearby tree branches, maybe the feral cats Leni habitually fed would feel the sting of empty bellies and whine, maybe the few stray cyclists to whom little

Alice had waved as they motored past on the bike path would wonder where that pretty girl and her strange mother had gone. But, otherwise, Leni's home would sink into the hungry mouth of the woods as though it had never stood upright and no one would be the wiser—not even the mailman, who had long since failed to deliver this route.

I took the lapse, the systematic failure to properly acknowledge human tragedy, personally. And I've described it to you now, in this way, and by these terms because I must take great care to rationalize and explain what happened five years later when I chanced upon Rick Merrick in a riverside bar. You have to understand: I wasn't looking for him. By that time, I'd largely written off hope of any justice for Leni or her daughter. I was in cognitive behavioral therapy, for Christ's sake. I had a steady girl, a hypoallergenic cat, and a lucrative work-from-home tech job to go with it. I had a goddamned library card with fines for overdue audio books on it. But that's not to say that I didn't simultaneously keep a detailed plan of action in wait. In the event that I ever came across the bastard or anyone affiliated with him, I was ready to set in motion a plan so strenuously considered that its steps were tattooed on my ever-loving mind.

It was one domino hitting the next the moment I recognized his name on the credit card receipt tucked under his foamed beer stein. It was his signature that drew my attention—a grand flourishing of ball-penmanship that suggested a wild bravado. It was so unreadable that I wondered what his name actually was. *Rick Merrick*, though it looked like a dolphin nudging the seafloor the way he signed it. *You have sealed your fate*, I thought, *with your own asshole signature*. I tucked my long baguette of a pocketbook beneath my arm, spun on my heel, and walked to my luxury sedan without a word spoken to my compatriots at the bar. When Rick Merrick emerged not three minutes later, I tailed his gray Honda to a shitty motel across the river. I waited to see which room he'd lumber into and then dialed a memorized number with a cell stashed inside my console.

Within about two hours, I was joined in the parking lot by a pair of professional miscreants for hire. They were trained to extract information from unwilling informants, and I'd engaged them in a long-term contract with the understanding that if I ever needed them, there'd be ten thousand dollars on the other side of a successful interrogation. If I never needed them, they'd have a free and easy five thousand sitting in their bank accounts. What could they lose? The miscreants knew what I wanted to know and they knew I had exactly zero qualms about the rough tactics required to extract it.

I took a considerable risk by waiting for them in my leather-upholstered boat of car on the dark side of the Ohio River. The idea was that I should be as far away as possible from what happened as to be reasonably free from any suspicion that might follow the violence required, but there were details I wished to review. Perhaps time had softened me. Maybe I'd become a micromanager in my maturity. I don't know. I told them to leave his balls alone. I told them to use the specter of McCallister if they had to, but to pose as cops for as long as possible. I told them there was a bonus in it if he was willing to lead them to Leni's grave. They went into the room, the pair of them quiet as leather on linoleum, and came out twenty minutes later with a map more detailed than my wildest hopes. At the end of a circuitous dotted ballpoint line on a Motel 6 pad, there was a careful square labeled *body*. Next to that square, there was a smaller square, also labeled *body*.

"He expressed regret," they told me, "but he didn't seem all that sorry."

"Why is he here?" I asked them.

"Mother's funeral," they told me. "He was in the pen a long time. Says he's trying to make amends."

I wired them the money from my car. And that was it. That should have been it. I followed Rick Merrick that night. He emerged from his room with a jacket over his head and threw himself into his Honda and sped off. I followed him the next night and the next and the next. I was invisible to him because he'd never registered my presence. He'd seen me—we'd been semi-introduced—but he'd never really seen me. Eventually, I dropped all precaution and sat next to him at the bar. Eventually, he took to telling strangers about the cops who'd tried to arrest him but they weren't cops and he knew that now, but what he didn't know was who was after him.

"Was it you?" he asked more than one man in the bar. "Was it because I fucked your girl that one time?"

He asked me. "Was it you? No, it couldn't have been you. Who the hell are you?"

I was nobody every time.

Eventually, he got so drunk so often that it was easy to follow him to the river and watch him fall in. I didn't even have to struggle with him. He went down and I kicked him over the embankment. He rolled log-like and then sank. I saw his head come up for air once, twice, gone. *Well*, I thought, *that takes care of that problem.* When I got home, my girlfriend asked me where I'd been night after night, a shade of anger in her voice, and I told her I'd been visiting with an old friend.

"Anyone I should know?" she asked.

"No," I told her. "Sometimes there's a reason old friends are old friends."

She nodded and we went to bed. Never discussed it again.

Despite the fact that McCallister was still a loose end, I let a sense of contentedness and ease slip into my living. I considered it futile to plot. I had no idea how to do somebody like him and never had. My only hope was to wait and pray that someone else did the job for me. There were other pushers in town. They may have been less organized than McCallister, but there were more and more of them all the time. Occasionally, one would off another and I'd read the paper with expectation, but our guy always seemed to emerge unscathed. The police called it a gang war, but it was more like prohibition hillbillies bombing competitor stills. Until some decent legislation found its way onto the books, the region would have to deal with some explosions. So, we waited and waited, pharmed up to the gills in the meantime.

On Christmas Eve of that year—like a special surprise from a morbid-as-hell Santa Claus—McCallister was found dead and deposited at the top of a heap of snow-covered rock at McCallister Gravel, butt of his own gun shoved someplace uncomfortable. They left the gruesome details out of the paper, the bullets ripping through his guts and escaping through the doorway of his head, but it was easy enough to draw the whole picture with my mind—a pleasure in which I indulged repeatedly. I raised a glass of red wine, toasted the Christmas tree, and that was that. The end of the Leni saga. That should have been the end.

The spot was one I think Leni would have liked. It was about a mile into the woods behind her trailer—or where her trailer once stood upright. By the time I finally got up my gumption to dig and know for sure, the burned-out husk was a rumpled pause in a sea of low green. I walked straight back and found the creek Rick Merrick had drawn in a deep blue line. The old bridge was right where he'd marked it and a series of Sycamores standing like white-sheeted ghosts in the woods. Now is probably the time when I should tell you that Leni was the first person to tell me she loved me. It had never occurred to me before that this was possible—that I could be loved.

"I love you, girl," she said. "I love you for just who you are."

She said it in the way you'd tell your sister you loved her right after she'd said something stupid and alienated the whole wedding party or insulted your parents' way of being in an accidental sort of way. Only, I'd just met her and we weren't even really related, and she didn't know I was gay—I didn't know I was gay—but she'd guessed it about me and wanted to make sure I knew it was OK.

"I love you too," I said. And I said it in the way that you silently thank someone for saving your life.

And so you can imagine why, when I got over myself and went into the woods to find her, I went there alone, armed only with a lame little gardening shovel. There were no officials present, no police task force, no investigative archeological team, not even my steady girl. I intended to pull back the dirt, make sure, and then leave them both there, Leni and her pretty daughter, Alice. This is the place I would visit when I wanted to pay my respects—at least I had that, I told myself. That's what my fifteen thousand had bought me. But then I dug and dug and dug and I didn't find anything. I dug up the creek and down the creek. I dug a thousand holes over the course of many years and never found a single human bone, nor any evidence of a burial of any kind.

I was left with several possibilities to mull with obsessive frequency. In the end, I decided that Rick Merrick may have been innocent of the murders or he may have been guilty of them. Either way, the map was bogus, probably constructed under duress from the miscreants, who wanted their bonus. Either way, I'd been had. I'd watched Rick Merrick die in the water, picturing the square next to the smaller square on the paper, while Leni and Alice, alive or dead, were somewhere else. When I called the miscreants, threatening exposure, they told me something I'd never known. Not only had Leni's husband confessed to murdering her and her daughter, he'd also confessed to doing some hits for McAllister, bumping junkies and lighting their squats on fire.

The next logical step is to tell you that Rick Merrick deserved it anyway. I could turn record of his convictions for domestic abuse like the peel of an apple in one long coil; I could lift the rock on his childhood and show you his baby sister running nude through the streets with half her hair burned off, I could trace with my finger the path of decay he wrought in the wide world. But what could it matter to you or anyone that a piece of trash stood by while another piece of trash sank in the Ohio River? So, I'll reveal instead that he knew me in that final moment. He didn't know who I was but he knew me as his murderer. And it felt like enough. And I was glad. Judge me if you will. The water in the creek near the plot I still regard as Leni's final resting place is as cloudy as the gray of her baby Alice's eyes. She would have been thirteen this year—no longer a little girl. I like to imagine her as the kind of teenager who smiles even though she might be feeling down. Leni would have raised her that way. She would have taught her girl to cling to the bright side, even though it can be tough to find one in a blue town.

Sole Survivor

Da kamen alsbald die Ratten und Mäuse aus allen Häusern hervorgekrochen und sammelten sich um ihn herum. Als er nun meinte, es wäre keine zurückgeblieben, ging er aus der Stadt hinaus in die Weser; der ganze Haufen folgte ihm nach, stürzte ins Wasser und ertrank.

Soon all the rats and mice came creeping out from all the houses and gathered around him. Once he knew that none of them were left behind, he went out of the city and into the Weser River; the whole pack followed him, plunged into the water, and drowned.

—*From the Brothers' Grimm, "German Legends"*

I.
The first time he comes, he's red like a bird. Stockinged and slight, the sharp prongs of his shoes pecking the pavers like beaks. He keeps his instrument tucked inside a bilious cape and withdraws it for the purposes of a demonstration. A sound like a thin, pinked ribbon unfurls and tugs the rodents from their slumber beneath the hay. They dance, the way rats dance, the sour flesh of

their feet flashing as they follow him through the gate, down the path to the Weser. There they dance a preamble to their deaths while the Mayor gladhands the deal: he'll pay, yes, he'll pay. He'll pay the Piper to drown the vermin one and all.

If the Mayor keeps his word, there will be no story to tell. And so perhaps we have him to thank for the spectacle of one hundred and thirty children dancing at water's edge and the deadly roil to follow. The Weser is not kind to those little bodies. It is, after all, under no obligation to show mercy. Only the Piper holds that claim. But he is dressed this time in green, the uniform of the hunter, and has no intention of shifting form. Maybe, if the townspeople were at home today, he might accept a doubled fee or an apology, but they're off worshipping martyrs, so he murders all of their children instead. Or, at least he thinks he does. As it turns out, he's left the job woefully incomplete.

II.

In the video, twelve dancers are arranged like sequined dollops on stage. They are all between five and seven years old and all of them have learned to hold their hands above their heads and wait for the music. The dancers will perform to Tchaikovsky's *Dance of the Sugar Plum Fairy*, but they are not sugar plum fairies; rather, they are rainbow sherbets. Were we to watch the show in its entirety, we would witness the spectacle of spumonis, frosty malts, root beer floats, and eggnogs executing halting pirouettes and plies—*Dancing for Desserts* is generously funded by the local dairy operation—but this recording features only the rainbow sherbets. In particular, the third dancer from the left. She doesn't know it now, but she's about to endure the first of many worst days of her life.

The tulle bunched beneath her tutu is orange, her tight elastic bodice is wrapped in green and pink satin, and her bun is topped with a heavily pinned swirl of flapping yellow sequins. She is ready for the dance to begin. She is un-nervous and prepared. She harbors a secret belief that this performance will secure her status as a dancer with some talent—or at least a little girl who follows direction well. She has shared this secret with no one and understands it as self-serious and strange. No one else in her class appears to care about dancing or following direction.

As the camera (manned shakily by grandpa's hand) pans from left to right, we will note the first dancer. She is the oldest and strongest. She will dutifully lead the line. The second dancer is the cutest. Her lacquered ringlets bounce appealingly. The third dancer is also a strong dancer, but is quiet and so her enthusiasm is suspect. She has been described as *morose*. She has difficulty holding her smile in the mirrored wall of the practice space. Her own mother has instructed her to *lighten up.* If the performance goes well, the third dancer from the left may stand the chance of dispelling, once and for all, the familial myth that she is the reincarnation of the great aunt who ruined her own wedding photos with her obscene frown.

The choreography is embarrassingly simple. It's not ballet, exactly, though there are a few easily recognizable moves peppered throughout. The idea is to march in a circular shape that gradually collapses until the line of dancers is reduced to a small hopping ring. Then they all run off the stage, run back on, and bow deeply. The only complication is the sudden reversal on the refrain. In rehearsal, this has proven to be a force of chaos and destruction. More than once, the instructor has threatened to murder all of the sherbets if they don't get it right. Above all, the third dancer from the left fears the shame of a failed reversal. Her mother, a widow whose overprotective tendencies have recently given way to abject exhaustion, has warned her against making the wrong move. *Whatever you do, don't make a fool of yourself —or me.*

III.

On the day the gunman rages through campus, the professor is late to class. It's odd, really, because the professor is never late to class. At times, she has wished she were the kind of teacher who could walk in late, the lecture hall abuzz with gossip, and fling a briefcase on a table, startling the students into silence. She has wished she were the type to offer no excuses for her tardiness and launch into a chalk-dusted screed of a lecture. But the truth is that she has never known herself to miss the start of a class by more than a minute. More often than not, in fact, she's in the room a quarter of an hour before class starts, tinkering with equipment and needlessly re-arranging sheets of paper.

She suspects that professorial lateness is chiefly a male prerogative. (Females are reluctant to give their classes one more reason to dismiss them.) But it is also a matter of her tenuous position at the university. She's a lecturer, not a tenured member of the faculty. (Lecturers are reluctant to give administrations one more reason to dismiss them.) And life has shown her repeatedly that if things can go wrong, they will. She's a pessimist. (Pessimists are reluctant to give the world one more reason to shit on them.)

All of this is to say that it would be highly unusual for her to walk into her classroom late. But, in addition to being a female, a lecturer, and a pessimist, the professor is also very unhappy. She has spent many years unraveling the knot in her heart that prevents her from having what other women her age have: husbands, children, steady jobs. But on this occasion, she has come in her sleep to the understanding that the knot isn't the problem; it's the whole damn ball of yarn. She wakes with a seamless knowledge that her insides are comprised of the wrong material: limp, weak, colorless. It's impossible to make a happy life out of insides like this.

She's only able to force herself out of bed when she remembers that she has promised to offer her students extra credit today. If she fails to appear, they'll be more likely to complain about their final grades and then an administrator will have at least three reasons to replace her. Full disclosure: it has been noted, recently, that she exerts *an uncomfortable presence* in the faculty lounge. No one ate the bright red sugar cookies she baked in an effort to counter the claim (perhaps red cookies suggest aggression or hostility rather than friendliness?). She's almost certain she's going to lose her position as she speeds to campus in her Acura.

Her usual lot is full, which means she'll be forced to circle like a starving vulture until a spot opens, a strategy that annoys her when she's the one walking back to her car. She hates the pressure, the sense that she's taking too long to unlock her door and buckle her seatbelt. *Get here on time and you won't have to wait for me to get situated*, she always wants to tell the vultures. She doesn't want anyone wanting to tell her such a thing today, so she decides in a huff to splurge on the pay-by-the-hour lot in the middle of campus. She'll blow twenty dollars by merely driving through the gate.

Relief spreads like a warmth in her brain, until the strap on her Mary Janes breaks on the way up the cobblestone hill. She has gym shoes in her desk, but her desk is on the other side of campus from the lecture hall where she teaches music theory to students who don't know what music theory is after studying it for fifteen weeks. *Fucking fuck all of them,* she thinks, as she limps back down the hill. Her office (in the basement, shared with some twenty-five other lecturers, smelling faintly of the chemical cleaning agents it contained when it was the janitor's store room) contains a giant, ticking wall clock, which tells her that she will be at least ten minutes late to class. If she's fifteen minutes late, half of her students will already be gone. All it will take is one complaint to bring down the axe. And then what will she do, move in with her mother?

By the time she reaches the hill with her ridiculous purple running shoes pounding the cobblestones, a stream of students is emerging from the lecture hall. *The bastards.* She's only ten minutes late. What happened to the fifteen-minute rule? Is that a real thing or an urban legend? As she nears the hall, she recognizes some of the students as her own, but there are also others in their midst—far too many students for the exodus to be confined to her class. The students meander down the cobblestone, chatting amiably. They don't seem to be headed anywhere in particular in any hurry. No one attempts to meet her eye. She has the very distinct sense that she is headed the wrong way; she should be at home, tending to her colorless insides.

IV.

The lone surviving girl is the quick subject of investigation. *What did she see and why didn't she try to do anything to stop it? Was she working in congress with the Piper?* She has no answer to these, or any, questions. She is only forgiven her failures because they think her deaf, mute, and lame. Her mother, an otherwise pious widow, is wise enough not to contradict them. And even if she did want to tell the truth, what would she say? *My daughter is only silent because she despises you for mocking her gait.* No, better to let the deaf mute of their imaginations tell the story with her fingertips, playing the piper's tune on a carrot and walking one hundred and thirty children spastic off the dinner table's edge. Better to let them assume her poor child incapable of malice or spite.

Later, when they are alone together, the mother pries out the whole sordid line. *Why would I follow those brats into the water? Why would I listen to such a foolish song? Why would I run and fetch you, if I knew my torment would soon end?* Of course, the girl could have rushed to the church to warn the people of the piper's return, she could have shouted or screamed the children out of their dreadful reverie, she could have at least tried, but she did not care if they drowned. It served them right, she now says, if they couldn't control their own bodies or minds. It served them right for never treating her with respect. *And now we'll be alone, Mommy, and no one will ever do us harm.*

The girl is not wrong. They are indeed alone together; their singular status makes them outsiders and targets of superstition, and while no one appears to wish them harm, her mother never forgets that her daughter is a monster. She lives her life in fear of discovery and retribution. All it would take is one knock on the door and her daughter's unthinking move to answer it, and they'd both be revealed as frauds. She waits for years, watches. She sleeps with her ear to the floor so that she might hear a visitor's light step in the night; then, out of exhaustion, she binds her daughter's hands and feet with ribbon and forbids her from leaving her room; then she seals the girl's ears with wax and forces her to carry a glass ball in her mouth. Nothing eases her worry.

Her nerves shorn by a decade of fear and silence, the mother finally endeavors to do the right thing, which is also the wrong thing. She walks her daughter to the banks of the Weser and shoves her into its winter churn. Bystanders will claim the young woman sang a song as she went down smooth as a spear—without any resistance or signs of fight or fear. It's the Piper, they'll say. He has found a way to overcome the defense of her impairment and has made his curse complete. All of the children born before Saint John and Paul's Day are now gone. The widow woman is a pious woman, but she is also wise. She holds her tongue again. The moral of her story, should one choose to discern it, is as cold as the river: *it's better to expose a monster than it is to harbor a sin.*

V.

Things go wrong almost immediately. The first dancer forgets the dreaded reversal. The second dancer follows her without hesitation, without pause. She is cute, remember, but not smart. The third dancer from the left is not a stickler for conformity, but she wants things to be done as they should be done. This may make her a *prude* (her mother's word), but it also makes her strong. It means she can think for herself. She makes the turn. Some of the dancers follow, others do not. There are conferences among the fourth through twelfth as the first, second, and third, continue to execute their steps. They all choose a leader—the oldest and the strongest— thereby rendering the third dancer from the left an errant, flouncing dessert.

It may seem as though she is ignorant of the choreography, it may seem as though she has made a grave mistake and has stuck stubbornly to her guns, but the truth is that she's the only dancer executing the dance properly; she's the only one following the rules. This is a truth that lodges painfully in her throat as she begins to cry, still faithfully conducting her march. She knows her mascara will run. She can sense her mother watching her from the audience, can hear her thoughts: *don't ruin it for everyone.* And so the man beckoning her from the side of the stage is a welcome sight. It is a relief to be called off. He wraps his jacket around her shoulders and they stand together for a moment, watching the travesty of *Dancing for Desserts,* one marching sherbet bumping into the next as they all turn their heads to see what has happened to the third dancer from the left. Where has she gone?

When they finally discover her, sitting on a bench outside the auditorium, nibbling at the soggy bottom of an ice cream cone, she will have no memory of the man. *I saw her leave with him, and I assumed he was one of yours,* the dance teacher will say, gesturing to the mother, the grandfather with the camcorder still strapped to his hand. *One of your people.* They will ask her time and time again, *Did he do anything to you? Did he touch you?* There's an answer somewhere inside her slick-bunned head, but they aren't asking her the right questions. What they should be asking her is how she came to know that she'd never be a dancer. It had happened in the instant that she realized none of the other girls had any talent and that *none of it mattered.*

The video of the recital becomes the subject of intense scrutiny. The moment the dancers split in their paths, the moment the third dancer seems to recognize someone beyond the red drape of the curtains, the moment she smiles and runs. *Who were you running to? Who was there?* But there was no one there. How can she explain that there was no one there? Later, the mother will strip the girl of her costume, unpin her hair, smear the makeup from her face, bathe her roughly, and review her body for signs of violation. Finding none, she will tell her daughter that she hopes she's happy. *Do you realize how much trouble you've caused? The next time this happens, I want you to do one thing for me, can you do that?* The girl nods. *Follow the goddamned leader.*

VI.

In her classroom, a fair portion of the students remain in their seats. Maybe twenty of the total seventy-five. The grade-grubbers. The kind of students who would remain seated through a hurricane if it meant they'd get the A. She's on the point of telling them that they may as well all leave—she's not going to teach the class with so many missing students—when the intercom voice makes his first confounding announcement: "Attention students. A threat has been perceived on campus. We request that you stay calm and follow Crisis Plan B, as detailed in your student handbook." The announcement is followed by a three-toned electronic scale. Bong, bong, bong. One of the seated students raises his hand and only lowers it when she finally thinks to call on him.

"Yes, James, what is it?"

"Is Crisis Plan B the one where we wait for you tell us what to do?"

James is never wrong. He could teach this class to the professor, and she'd learn from him. He has memorized the textbook and can quote from her masters thesis, if prompted. On the first day of class, he told her he was proficient in twenty-seven instruments, but he was aiming for an even number. He was thinking of taking up harmonica. Was that stupid? How would that look on his resume? The professor remembers telling James that the harmonica would indeed look stupid; if he wanted to impress potential employers, he should call it a blues harp instead. He did not detect her sarcasm, and she was helpless to correct their toxic dynamic. Now, she asks him if he knows what Crisis Plan A is all about.

"That's the one where we evacuate immediately and return to our dorms or places of residence."

"That voice clearly said Plan B, did it not?"

A student on her left pipes up. "That's why we're sitting here waiting for you to show up and tell us what to do. He's already told us to do Plan B three times."

"Right," she says. "I'm sorry I'm late. I've never been late for a class in my life. I slept in and then my shoe broke. That's why I'm wearing these sneakers." She looks down at her shoes. The spring-like structures built into the soles make her feel like a clown athlete. Real athletes don't need springs to help them walk up hills; real athletes don't buy off-brand shoes on clearance at the drug store. Only clown athletes do that.

"You'd think I'd have some training for events like these, but there's nothing like that for professors in my position," she says. She snorts. "I guess they expect us to inflate our grades enough to avoid being shot in the head. Anyway, I'm sure it's a glitch in the system. If it were a real threat, campus police would be here, right? I came up the hill a minute ago, and I didn't see any sign of them."

Several students stand and rush up the carpeted ramp to the exits at the back of the room, some leaving their belongings at their desks. "Sorry," she calls after them. "That was a dumb thing to say. I'm a little off today." She smacks the side of her head like there's a loose stone rattling inside and she can pop it out the opposite ear if she tries.

James, one the final holdouts, rises slowly and puts his arms through the straps of his neon backpack. "You don't have any clue what we're supposed to do," he says. It's a question, but it's also a statement; more importantly, it's the most direct approach he has ever taken with her. She knows she has upset him, and that was wrong, but the truth is that they're all on their own. He may as well learn that lesson now and make the trip to class worthwhile.

"Go, if you want," she says. "It won't impact your grade."

"I think I'll go."

"Great, go. Frankly, I wonder why you didn't follow the others."

The intercom voice interrupts with his second confounding missive. "Attention students. The perceived threat level has been raised to Status Orange." The three-toned scale follows. Bong, bong, bong.

"Oh, for Christ's sake," she says. This is the first and only time she's ever taken the Lord's name in vain in the presence of students. It's a Jesuit institution and though she's not religious herself, she doesn't want to give the powers-that-be one more reason to oust her. "What in the hell is Status Orange supposed to be?"

The paralyzed shrimp to James's left raises his smartphone in the air. "It means we await further instruction," he says.

She becomes aware of the scent of sulfur, faint plumes of smoke licking the undersides of the rear doors and is hit with the nauseating understanding that her dithering has endangered them all. If they all die, it will be her fault they've all died.

"No," she says. "It means we hide. Right now."

Despite her earnest attempts to herd her students toward and through the door she knows is hidden behind the giant, stacked chalkboards at the front of the classroom, they all defy her. Instead, they follow James, who reveals himself as their true leader and tells her to go to hell. He drops his backpack and runs. All of her remaining students follow suit, disappearing through the heavy doors at the back.

"There's something terrible happening out there," she yells after them.

She briefly considers following James too, attempting to re-assert herself as a leader, but then decides she'll only slow them down. It would be better if they didn't have to worry about her. Behind the chalkboards, a short hall leads to an anteroom where only faculty are allowed. It's a bland, windowless space. Only a very lonely person would spend any time here, which is why it's the perfect place for her lunch, regularly conducted directly after class and comprised of egg salad and chocolate milk. She feels perfectly at home here and utterly safe. Then the intercom voice interrupts to offer his first clear instruction of the ordeal. "A definitive threat has been perceived," he says. "Proceed to the nearest exit and evacuate immediately." Bong, bong, bong.

"Run if you want to run," the professor says to herself. She checks herself for the impulse, but it isn't there. She wants to stay. It's only when she hears the tapping of gunfire that she remembers her smartphone in her pocket. Her mother texts her as she holds the phone in her hand. *Don't be a hero! Get the hell out of there now!* And then, *Are you OK?* And then, *They're shooting kids in there. Do you know that?* And then, *They don't pay you enough to take a bullet!* She tells her mother too much, she decides. That's the problem. In the future, she'll be more careful to withhold. She'll tell her mother that teaching is the fire in her eye. She'll tell her it's her true calling. It doesn't matter what she gets paid if she loves what she does.

When the smoke clears and the authorities discover her unharmed, sitting comfortably in a cold off-white room not even the janitor seems to know about, there will be questions: *Why didn't you leave with your students? Why didn't you attempt to protect the twelve who stayed? Why were you late today? How did you manage to survive?* And she will have good answers for none of them. It's possible she may not survive, of course. She may be harmed. The lunatic roving the halls in his green duster—the one with the bone to pick with feminists, the one who felt lonely in the dining hall, or the one who spent too much time on the internet playing war games—might be aware of this intermediary space, this non-classroom/non-non-classroom. It's possible he's worked it into his attack plan: drive the students down the funnel of the lecture hall and pick them off once they're confined and easy to target. These shooter kids aren't often very good marksmen. They have to make allowances for the fact that their training is only in their minds.

If he finds only her, he's likely to be disappointed. She'll be sitting on a deflated couch, feet propped up on a molded plastic chair, while texting her mother. *Do you think you could take care of the cats for a while?* She'll be as likely to invite his bullet as she will be to fear it. If he asks her a question—*Why didn't you leave while you still had the chance?*—she'll probably feel obliged to answer, but she may not. What does she owe this pimply-faced lout? No, better to let him deal with the disconcertion of an unafraid and unfleeing victim. Let that be her last gift to the planet—adult woman disaffection in the face of teenaged male disaffection.

The gunfire is closer and it quickens her heart, brings sweat into her sleeves. Despite her fear, she still fully intends to dismiss the threat and the almost overwhelming temptation to bolt. The intercom voice begins an announcement—"Attention students"—and then stops. The three-toned scale bongs. Bong, bong, bong. It's like a song, she realizes, luring the few remaining students and faculty members out of their hiding places and into the open. It's the Pied Piper of poor campus crisis planning. What was the lesson of that story? Always pay your bills, never follow the leader, avoid suspicious street musicians?

The way it was told by her mother, whose text messages have quickly evolved from panic and concern to frustration and resentment—*Why are you doing this to me? What did I do to deserve this? Get out of there!*—it was a threatening kind of warning that shifted with the violence of her moods. *Embarrass me in front of strangers again and I'll be entitled to punish you endlessly.* Or, *it is better to die than to stand out in a crowd.* Or, *sooner or later, you'll get what you deserve.* Her mother had a tendency of writing mother characters into all of the old fairy tales she told the professor as a child. The mother characters weren't always heroes (her attempt at even-handedness?), but they always stole the show. The mother character might be one of the main reasons the professor is not a mother.

Her smartphone now tells her that a lone gunman is prowling the halls. He's shooting at anyone in sight. The police can't get to him because he has barricaded the front doors and placed explosives around some or all of the windows and doors. She considers ducking behind the couch but doesn't want to be caught that way—cowering. She wants to be the one who throws this guy off with her seeming nonchalance. *Go ahead. I've been waiting for this moment all my life.* She unties the laces on her awful purple shoes and settles in for the long haul, wedging a lumpy pillow behind her back. She resolves to conserve battery power and puts her phone in do-not-disturb mode, whatever that means, and tilts back her head. When the gunman flings open the door to the hidden anteroom, she won't even be surprised. She'll be napping, she thinks. Then, eight hours later, when the stress of appearing nonchalant has reduced her to an exhausted, huddled mass, she actually does manage to sleep.

A day has passed. The crisis has resolved itself without her knowledge or awareness. She tries to turn on her phone, but it refuses, battery dead. The device is as useless as a chalk eraser to her. It takes her a few hours of consideration and re-consideration, but she finally musters the courage to emerge. Her fear is not that the gunman will still be waiting for her, but rather that she'll catch a policeman off guard and be shot mistakenly. There's a headline she does not wish to court. CONTINGENT FACULTY SLAIN BY FRIENDLY FIRE. Her slow progress down the back stairway is marred by no signs of great violence. There are no pools of blood or broken glass. Once outside, she can see that all of the activity is focused on the front of the building. A herd of reporters stands under bright lights and yellow police tape flaps in the wind.

As she makes her way down the cobblestone, no one tries to stop her for questioning. No one appears to notice her at all. By the time she makes it to her usual lot and realizes that her Acura is parked in the pay-by-the-hour lot, her day has taken on the familiar hue of the chronic frustrations in her life. Now she'll have to pay at least fifty dollars to get her car off campus. She could contest the fee, but then she'd have to explain that she'd been sleeping in the lecture hall while a crazy person riddled the places with bullets. Yes, that's right, she'd slept through the worst tragedy of her life. What's the moral of the story? *Be careful where you lounge; it may be more sleep-inducing than it first appears.* When she arrives home, it's clear her mother has not been by to feed the cats. They swarm her, as though she's been gone for months, and then evade her touch. She dumps a full bag of kibble on the kitchen floor, fills a giant soup pot with fresh water for them, and marches up the stairs to take a shower.

She considers turning on the NPR as she lets the water steam the mirror, her usual habit, but she's not prepared to hear any of the details regarding the shooting: the body count; the names of the dead, which are likely to include a few of her own students, if not all of the twelve who left her hiding and alone in the lecture hall; the early tales of professorial heroism, her colleagues who sacrificed themselves. She's not prepared to hear her own name among those who are missing or presumed dead. Most of all, she's not prepared to hear her mother's weeping reprisals. *I told her to get out of there.* She steps into the scald of the water, that voice still ringing in her head. *I told her to find another line of work. Something where she didn't have to deal with people. You'd be appalled to know what they pay her. A Ph.D. shopping at Goodwill for work clothes. Can you imagine?*

It is then that it comes to her. She will leave. She will wash her body, toss her clothes and her shoes into the neighbor's trash, and use the presumption of her death or traumatization to give herself a head-start on anyone who might want to find her. She steps into the water, feels her old self falling away, and catches herself on the other side of herself humming a strange little three-toned tune. Bong, bong, bong.

VII.

Rest assured, the mother has regrets. There is a way of seeing the story that makes it seem like she's the villain. But she has always prided herself on her ability to overcome hardship. She won't let the loss of the daughter slow her down. Now that she's free from the embarrassment of her charge, she considers remarrying. She considers radically revising her appearance. She considers an occupation that might lead her out of the house. She waits a month (she has no wish to appear unfeeling) and emerges a changed woman, but every time she sets foot on the other side of the gate, she finds herself inexplicably drawn to the little cobblestone road down by the river. Try as she might, she cannot deviate from this path.

After trying and failing for months to arrive anywhere else, she finally walks into the water and is never seen or heard from again. Bystanders will claim that she showed signs of distress as she moved through the water, reaching back to the banks with her arms while her legs marched her steadily forward. It was the strangest thing, they will say, but she seemed as though she were dancing.

WHAT GOOD ARE YOU?

This morning I walked my daughter May's new bed up three flights of stairs backwards and solo. It was well past time to sacrifice her crib for a twin, but she's my only, and, if I'm honest, I liked her contained at night. Her main objection to the switch was metaphorical: she blocked me on the landing when I didn't have a good answer to the question of why I'd separated the twins. I had to buy her off with my hidden can of Pringles. The mattress was easy. I slid it like an enormous slice of bread into an apartment-sized toaster. The box spring was another story. I sheared off a curl of wallpaper the length of a semi and hid the evidence of my crime at the bottom of the communal trash.

And now, at last, I'm in bed. There's somebody imaginary in here with me who cares or at least pretends to care. Today, it's somebody with highly skilled hands. He's unraveling my hamstrings. Thread by thread. He's kneading my ass like a stalled heart. He tells me I have too much tension in my spine. He gets me in the back, fingers all a flutter. He recommends treatments involving steam and mud and a pedicure and chemical peels. I ask him what he does afterhours. At his price, he says, there's not enough room for him in my mind. This is the way it goes: wrong every way it could. I tell the pillow and the sheets my legs are killing me. I lean my head over the side of the mattress and tell the carpet. I tell its stains.

"It isn't fair," I say. "Give me at least the capacity to imagine. Is that too much to ask?"

I sense somebody watching me before I spot May's red shoes on the carpet.

"My legs are killing me after moving your new bed into your room," I say.

She's four, so her present willingness to extend sympathy consists of eye contact. She checks me for sarcasm. Squints her eyes, screws up her mouth. I notice she's got some kind of junk on her face. Something pink, resembling paste, spread in circles on each of her cheeks. "Playing make-up?" I ask. She nods. She wants to know how to get gum out of hair without cutting.

"Do you have gum in your hair?" I ask.

"No," she says.

She spins Malibu Barbie around her thumb by the hair.

"Does she?"

She grips Barbie by the legs and shakes her rubber head at me.

"Peanut butter," I say. "Grandma did a hot iron once on me. Peanut butter is better."

"Do we have any?"

"We switched to almond butter," I say. "Have you ever seen the inside of a Barbie head?"

We squeeze Malibu's head off and force her forehead through her neck. We laugh at the stubs of hair inside and the mouth that looks like an asshole. We make her body dance on the bed, hunt wildly for her head on the nightstand. She finds an apple core, a pair of sunglasses, a paperclip. "I'm right here!" the head says. "Right here!"

In Tennessee today, a dog died curiously. I find these things out on the news. He was chewing his tail and then he was dead. The family couldn't figure it. When the vet opened his stomach, there were twenty-eight golf balls inside. "I'm the one who trained him to chase those balls," said the father of the family. "There is such a thing as training a dog too well. I see that now." We take what lessons we can.

Ray calls from work, and I'm in the middle of convincing somebody imaginary I'm eccentric. Somebody with actual muscles. *My drapes are made completely of negligées*, I'm saying, *and my husband says he doesn't consider it cheating.* Ray wants to know what to expect when he gets home because he's hungry. He likes to pretend I'm the kind of wife who prepares for him. He knows he's only pretending. I unprepared May's father right out of the state.

"I'm in the middle of something," I say. "Jesus Christ."

"Chicken?" he asks.

"You think so?" I say. "Somebody's telling me my thighs are diamond-plated."

"Sounds pretty good."

"Oh, it is."

In my mind, I'm sashaying around the room. Every step is like pulling a world of sex into rotation. With a flick of my hips, I can floor the jaws of a thousand men on the other side of the planet.

"What are you doing?"

"Pretending I'm not doing what I'm doing."

"Okay. What aren't you doing?"

"Do you think it's possible for your mind to be more stupid than you actually are?"

"Jules?"

"Chinese. We're having Chinese for dinner."

"I might just do chicken here, then."

"Suit yourself."

"What do you mean you're stupid?"

I'm quiet until he hangs up.

May and I do Chinese without Ray. She gets upset when I pry his fortune cookie open with my teeth and spit the slip of paper into my palm. "That's his," she says. Her sense of territory rivals my own. We label our half-empty cups of juice in the fridge.

"I'm a horse, what do you expect?" I ask her.

"What's he?"

We consult the menu. A monkey. Headstrong and chatty. Compatible with rats and dragons.

"Shit," I say. "I should have consulted this before I agreed to the whole marriage thing."

We read the fortune. *What is behind you is never ahead of you*, it says. "Boring," we say like snotty teenagers—high pitch on the first syllable, low on the second, a sarcastic teeter-totter of a word. We play with the egg-drop soup, let spoonfuls glop into the plastic container from greater and greater heights. "His fortunes are always so boring," I say. May considers this, stirs some plum sauce into some sweet and sour into some soy sauce.

"Does Ray have a bald spot?" she asks.

"In the future, he may," I say. "And this is why we eat his cookie."

She consults her own scalp.

"I will never eat your cookie," I say.

In Florida, a seventy-eight year-old man fends off an alligator. They have him on the news with the loafer he thrust against the animal's beak. If he could do this much with only a shoe, just think what you could do with all the parts that make up a smile.

Ray is home at nine. Late. I was planning on looking funny when he came in, painting my toenails waitress-red, upside-down on the expensive couch where it's dangerous. I even considered squeezing into May's soccer tee-shirt. Number eight. One sexy number. Instead, he walks in on me staring into his sock drawer.

"Hello," he says. "Are you in there?"

"Chinese is in the fridge," I say. "We read your fortune. It was boring again."

"I told you about the chicken. What are you up to?"

The truth is that I have counted sixteen pairs of the same bland tube socks and am transfixed by the spectacle of the balls fastidiously stacked in rows of four. When does he find the time to make sure the red stitching in each toe faces outward? How does he do it? It's like he's created a private footwear choir and it's in there waiting for the cue to sing. I assume it would do patriotic numbers, masculine tunes scented with dryer sheets.

"You have some really lame socks," I say.

"What's wrong with my socks?"

"I'll try to love you anyway."

"Is this another trick?"

"Probably."

We assume the customary positions on the bed: his back to the headboard, mine to the footboard. He loosens his tie while I get at his shoes. This same routine happens every day because it has happened every day for three years. This is what the married versions of us do. The unmarried versions did the same, only they had something to sell. He tells me about a woman at work, an ancient telemarketer going through chemotherapy.

Penny. He has sympathy for the woman. I have sympathy too because Ray's job is all that's keeping me from having a real job—one where I'd have to show up during the week and worry about hair.

"They've got all kinds of toxins going into her," he says. "Her waste is a biohazard. She can't be around kids."

"How sad," I say. "Does she like children?"

"That's not the point."

"What about pets? Can she have pets?"

"Look, the point is, there's no decent ventilation in the place, so the air from the bathroom goes chugging through the pipes, spurting through the vents over the cubicles."

Ray is wearing the seventeenth pair of bland tube socks. The red stitching is twisted into a vertical position at the toe. I poke at the errant bulge of fabric there. "Doesn't this bother you?"

"Are you listening to me?" He pulls his feet beneath his thighs.

"So, what happens with the pipes again?"

The fact that I'm talking to my husband about toxic shit does not escape me. There's some part of me that is pleased with his candor. I imagine that before I married Ray, I imagined this kind of scenario as fantastical. What a marvel, the husband who can say anything and will say anything. God love a man who won't spare your virgin ears. But now, now that it's literal shit we're talking about, I don't know.

"You can imagine what happens. The smell. There's nothing anyone can do about it," he says.

"Nothing?"

"Well, you can't *say* anything."

"Why not?"

"The woman has cancer, for Christ's sake."

"Right. Totally inappropriate idea."
We stare at opposite ends of the bed.
"There's Chinese?" he says.
"It's all yours, baby."

The children in California have been eating poison. It's true. They can't keep the candy off the shelves, despite proof that it contains dangerously high levels of lead. Especially popular are the apple yaw-yaws, a *tamarindo* jellied fruit candy. If you think the worst news is poison disguised as candy, you've got another thing coming.

It's two in the morning and I know May will be up in a few hours, but I'm forcing Ray to watch the entirety of a reality show about surviving naked around pointy sticks. He smokes a rare cigarette in bed, ashing into a toy dump truck left by one of May's boy friends in his pillowcase. "What were they doing in here together?" he says.

"They play in here sometimes."

"Doesn't that worry you?"

"Why should it?"

He opens the night table drawer, exposing a damning heap of condoms. A vertical stack expands like a string of photos out of a wallet, revealing the bulbous vibrator.

"They don't care about that stuff," I say.

He ashes into the dump truck. "There are boundaries, Jules," he says.

"You're too private," I say.

"I'm normal."

"And I'm a freak. A freaking sexual freak." I snatch the cigarette and smoke more than my fair share of it, exhaling down my chin and between my breasts. He feigns annoyance. "What do you fantasize about, Ray?"

I say. This is not the first time I have asked this question. He calls it *the* question. I ask *the* question in my best schoolgirl voice. I ask it again, "What do *you* fantasize about?" And again, "What *do* you fantasize about?"

"You."

"But what do you *fantasize* about?"

He leans over the side of the bed and makes a grab for the condoms. The truck drives into his crotch and leans there. I want to drive it up his chest, make it skid in the hair there, radio for help.

"Come on," I say. "Play along."

He heaves himself upright. "Okay. Underage teens washing cars."

"Funny. God, I love you."

"I fantasize about you," he says. He says the familiar words, "You, you, you, you, you." He slings the condoms around his neck like a boa, raises a coquette eyebrow. "I sit at my desk and imagine what you're doing here. Maybe you're leaning over the kitchen table to yell at May in the living room. Your skirt lifts in the back as you lean, just exposing the rim of your underwear."

"You fantasize about my ass?"

"Fine," he says, grabs the cigarette and crushes it into the truck.

"It's hard to think of myself that way—of my ass," I say.

"It's not hard for me to think of your ass."

"Really? My ass?"

The show finally ends with the final contestant carted off in an ambulance and Ray leans across me to close the laptop, plastering a sneaky kiss on me. My mouth moves beneath this sneaky kiss. I want to tell him something, maybe make him ask me what it is that I fantasize about. I want him to make me tell him, force it out of me. I want him to make me tell him the truth. I want to feel it there, the shape of the word on my tongue, round and full: *more, more, more.* But then he's already asking if I'll get the light.

A former porn star is battling the spread of AIDS in the adult movie industry. Her titles include "Jail Bait" and "Captain Lust and the Pirate Women." Says a friend and fellow former actor, "She is basically the Mother Teresa of porn." The lesson here is we're all good for something, even if we're bad. What good are you?

I call Leslie after I get May off to pre-school. There was trouble getting the lunch into the bag, getting the bag into the kid's hand, getting the kid and the bag into the car. "I refuse to eat almond butter," May was saying, like she had standards to uphold, like it was political. And I started thinking, then, about getting involved with a hot tub. I kept thinking about it. Leslie seemed like the right person to explain this to over the phone. She's always been the kind of woman who really *gets* hot tubs. She *gets* memberships to spas, *gets* cocktails and spontaneous pixie cuts. And she's my only post-baby friend.

"I'm thinking of having an affair with myself," I say. She doesn't hear me right, tells me to shut up and listen to her for once. Leslie is the kind of woman you pay attention to or else. She puts her lipstick on in a way that says *don't mess with me.* Nut-red, serious stuff.

"Look, Jules," she says. "You're only thinking about this because you've just realized you're married. It doesn't hit you until you're too far into it."

"I want to turn me on," I say. "Tickle my fancy."

"What does May say?"

"May?"

"What does your daughter say about the man you married?"

"May loves Ray. Why?"

"Are you pregnant?"

"Oh, of *course* I am."

I flick on the TV while she's talking, telling me about my options. "Don't fall for those pregnancy help centers," she says. "There's just a bunch of Christians in there, waiting to reform you. Did I ever tell you how that happened to me once?"

I tell her it sounds awful. I tell her I can only imagine. There's a show on about exercise. A man is selling a machine that works out for you, shoots electrical current through your muscles, causing them to clench without any effort of your own. All of the women in the show are wearing yellow spandex, and all of them are smiling because they can wear yellow spandex. And it's their *job.*

"They tried to read me passages out of the Bible," Leslie says.

"What did you do?"

"What do you think I did?"

There is a long pause that tells me I'm supposed to get something. Leslie doesn't have kids. She hates them. Probably, she told those Christians where to stick their Bibles. The yellow spandex girls are working out while they read magazines beside a pool shaped like a jellybean. Old women are doing it with their feet up on recliners. Moms and dads are doing it while they watch the kids play in the yard. They drink soda and get abs at the same time. They clench and clench and clench.

"You know I'm not really pregnant, right?" I say.

"I sure as hell hope not," she says.

I notice, as I look in the mirror, that my eyebrows have been doing something funny lately. It's a definite trend. They're conspiring together to make me look sad. Or is that a grimace? "I've got to go, dear," I say to Leslie. "I think it's an eyebrow emergency."

Then I decide to take off all my clothes and stand naked in the hall mirror. Sometimes, you have to do this just to see. I pull off my shirt, throw it on the table, and there's a large, black insect on the inside of it—a spider, but heftier somehow. Has it been inside my shirt all day? How does something like that even happen? Its cluster of eyes is large enough that I can discern its indecision. It wants to run, but it's frozen. My mouth tightens. Without looking in the mirror, I know that I'm making the face that I make when something painful happens to someone else. I first made this face when my high school boyfriend took a softball to the groin. Now, I must make it a thousand times a day—when people are rude to cashiers, when I have to hang up on sales calls, when my daughter pleads with me to eat a bag of mini marshmallows or download a crappy new app. Somehow, I must halt the creep of this face.

"You're not wanted here," I say to the bug, and it dies.

Just like that. Dead.

I'm still plucking my misbehaving eyebrows when May walks into the bedroom at three. Either the carpool ran late or she's been in the house for an hour without me knowing it. She tells me I'm bloated. "You look like a fat, lazy fish," she says. She has remote controls in the pockets of her purple dress. The pockets are big white hearts. I have no memory of purchasing this garment.

"Fish aren't fat," I say.

"Yes they are." She inflates her cheeks, makes fins out of her ears.

"You're right. I'm a fat, lazy fish."

"I want to play at Natalie's."

"Leave the remotes."

"They're not remotes; they're Tasers."

"Oh yeah?"

She shoots me with one. I collapse on the bed, shudder like I'm in a seizure.

"Wake up, lady," May says. "You're giving me a cornea."

"Coronary," I say and then expire.

She shakes my shoulders, wags my head by the jaw, but I'm gone; it's too late for me. I hear her leave before I open my eyes. Next door, Natalie's mom opens on the first knock. I hear her say she's happy May and her daughter get along so well, but they've spent the whole day together at school. "Don't you want to spend some time with your own family?" she asks.

"No, not really," says May.

"How's your mother feeling?" asks Natalie's mom. I realize I don't know her first name, that I've called her *Natalie's mom* for five years, that she calls me *Julie*, which I despise. We share a long wall and overhear both kitchen and bathroom activities, which means we know both everything and nothing about each other. She has borrowed one item from me: a single, large brown egg. She returned it with eleven others. Organic. Fancy eggs. In an anomalous spate of baking, I once borrowed a flour sifter from her. I washed it and she told me to keep it, it was ruined. "I can see that you've left it in the water," she said. I felt like an ass, a child. I decided to forget about it.

From my post on the bed, arms flung over my head and legs spread, I hear Natalie's mom asking my child what she did at school today and that's when I begin to wonder what happens when these sorts of indiscretions pile up. Eventually, will all of the Natalie's moms of my life show up and make me pay for my sins? It seems highly likely that they will. One of these days, they'll line up with their evidence—the eyeballs poked without apology, the muddied shoes, the bad tips, the fenders bent—and stage a counterassault. Their leader—I can see her now—will press the buzzer and lie in wait. She'll be holding one hand over her eye, still red and irritated years after the accidental entry of my finger, and in the other hand, she'll hold a torch.

She, and all of the other women I've offended, will threaten to burn me out. But, they'll be easy to ignore, even despite the flames, because someone will be whispering in my ear. He'll be telling me it's possible to ignore everything forever. *You've got the right disposition for it*, he'll say. *You're more self-absorbed than anyone thinks.* He'll have the perfect machine for me—a little box that sends electrical currents straight into the heart, makes it stop whatever it's doing in there.

In a September road-rage incident in Salt Lake City, a woman sped by in a blocked-off lane to get around a motorist on the interstate. She then rolled down her window and screamed at him. The man made an obscene hand gesture. The woman then pulled out a .357-caliber revolver, shot off the tip of his middle finger, and sped away. Lesson: where there's give, there's take.

It may be true that once you've been with someone one way, you can't be another way without also becoming a liar. You can't tell your husband what you want without saying also, *this me that you know, she isn't really me. I'm the no-good girl. And here you thought I was a peach.* A scream when it comes in bed, in the kind of bed where there is no screaming, where there is no sound at all that is a voice, can only be heard as fear. It might be more accurately called pleasure, but then. There is too much explaining to do. Tonight, I decide to tell Ray a bedtime story. This is another one of our routines. A new story every time, has to be totally original, no repeats or cameos. I pull the sheet under his arms, smooth it over his belly, and run my finger down the length of his nose.

"Listen," I tell him. "Once upon a time there was this girl." I tell him about the girl who loves birds. She loves them more than can be spoken. She loves them more than love. She begins by wanting only to touch them. She wants to feel their feathers, the fine weight of their bones. Once she learns how to make them let her touch them, she wants more. She wants to hold them. The small ones, she wants to hold completely in her hands. Once she learns how to make them let her hold them, she wants to keep them in her mouth. She gathers bird after bird and places them inside, giving each the perch of a tooth.

"The thing is," I say, "she can never tell anyone about it, even though she wants to. She's afraid if she opens her mouth, they'll remember to fly. She loves the birds so much she starves."

"That's depressing," says Ray. "Am I supposed to get something?"

"I'm depressed."

"May told me."

"May told you what?"

"She said you stay in bed too much. You're boring."

"I don't want to be boring."

"Do something."

"Like what?"

"Do something good."

I pull the pillow from beneath Ray's head and place it over my own face. Someone should give me an award for doing this good deed.

I show up at Natalie's mom's house with a cake. It's an upside-down cake. Nectarine. She says she doesn't eat cake, only pie. She says she doesn't let her kids eat any sugar because they bounce off the walls. I think about inviting her kids over and feeding them cheap, refined sugar, straight out of the sack. I leave the cake beside the building's mailboxes with paper plates and a knife. When I go to check my mail later, the cake and plates are still there. The knife is gone.

Ray gets me a job by talking to an old friend of his and I decide to resent him for it. And it's not because it shows he doesn't trust me to go out and get a job on my own. I wouldn't—he's got me there. And it's not because I don't want the job. I do—everyone agrees it will be good for me. I resent him for it because it's the kind of job that only happens on the weekends, when everyone else is grilling. I decide in advance that I'll be good at my sad, weekend job. I'll be the model employee, an officious human woman. I wear the nametag I'm planning to lose soon—JULES BASTIAN MERCHANDISE—right above my left breast on my turkey-red vest. And I gear up to try my best to sell home products I know very little about to people who don't really need them. I muster up the will to try to make people feel like they are getting a good deal. "Can I help you?" I say to myself in the car. "Home accessories are my specialty."

When I say this sort of thing to actual customers, though, I seem only to confuse and anger them. Of a pair of Edison bulbs in a clear plastic wrap, I tell a woman, "Those are *amazing*. They will last forever. And I mean forever." Of the outdoor placemats made of recycled plastic beads, I tell another woman, "Those are killer mats." Neither of these exchanges results in sales. It all comes to a head when I try to help an older man in a mesh trucker hat decide between wooden and ceramic napkin rings.

"Tough call," I say. "Go with your gut."

He slips the rings back on the rack and appraises me. "You don't know shit about shit," he says.

He walks down the aisle and out the automatic doors. I think about this for hours, standing silently in the aisles I'm responsible for re-stocking. Really? Shit about shit?

I eat lunch in the employee lounge. Almond butter on crackers. There's no table in the lounge, but there are lockers and motivational posters. One says, simply, *SMILE*. Big white block print on a black background. *SMILE*. I lean on the lockers and think about cigarettes. If I start, I'll have something to do on these breaks and then maybe I can be upset about having to quit. The novelty of the pay phone with the reminder tacked above—*personal calls five minute maximum*—intrigues me enough to slide my cell out of my pants and dig up Leslie's number. She picks up on the first ring, and I say, "Do you think it's true that smiling makes you happy even if you're not?"

"Are you smiling right now?" she asks.

"Yes."

"There you have it."

"Are you smiling?"

"Wait, who is this? I don't know this number."

I'm not sure I know who or what I am, but I know that I'm about to walk out on my job on the first day. It's too much, these emotional directives. Who do they think they are, telling my face what to do? As I leave the store, I play a little motivational game of my own. I set a steady pace as I cross the sales floor. I challenge myself to keep this pace at all costs. No matter what happens. No matter how many afterthoughts I know I'll have. They can all come after me, the army of managers with their walkie-talkies. They can cling to my legs, and I will drag them along. Nothing can stop me. When my feet hit the sensory mat of the automatic door, I hold my pace, grazing the doors as they split.

In the parking lot, though, I'm wholly consumed by the spectacle of a woman trying and failing to get her kid and a cart full of junk into her shitty Honda. Small items drop from her purse—a brush, some gum, a wad of Kleenex—as she leans into the car to shove her boy into his carseat by the head.

"Here," I say. I grab a bag. "Let me help you with this."

"No," she says.

"Why? I'm not going to steal from you. I work here."

She points her car key at my face. "I'm warning you," she says.

"You're warning me? Against doing my job?"

There are probably five, six plastic bags left in her cart. I figure, if I grab with both hands, I can get four into her hatchback before she stops me. There's a part of me that can understand why she'd be hostile, but come on. Her shirt is buttoned wrong, and I can see she's been crying. The kid is losing his mind inside the car, raging at the straps on his carseat like they're on fire. I make quick work of the bags. While my head's inside, arranging them, he pauses in his wail and eyeballs me.

"Hi guy," I say. "Give your mom a break, will you?"

He cracks a smile, and my heart swells. Maybe this is what I was meant to do with my life: half-assedly alleviate the despair of other mothers. My sense of accomplishment is temporary. Once the bags are in the car and the hatch is shut, my new mission in life un-hatches and unloads. She starts out casually enough, but soon she's throwing, rather than placing. And then she's tearing and flinging, trashing and stomping. Paper plates spin out of their tubes of plastic and lamp oil runs in heavy lines. Juice boxes and throwaway Tupperware, cheap cheese things and diapers—the junk of the ordinary household flung wild. The diapers. A thousand diapers. They're impossible to catch and get back into the sack. A person could spend a lifetime under cars and she'd never get them all back.

"Stop it," I say. "Look what you're doing to us!"

I don't know how the helping becomes fighting, but there's a struggle, a terrible, slapping dance that takes us to the ground when we both lose our footing in her groceries. After the collapse, we stay down, breathing, the wind taking her cart away. Somehow, we manage to hold each other. Little known fact: you can't even tell you're in a parking lot when it's the size of Kansas, and you're on the ground looking up. There's a blue sky above like they always want it to be in songs. And here I am, sharing this moment with the one person who probably understands me better than I understand myself. This is as close as I'm ever getting to spiritual transcendence.

A Pennsylvania woman pleaded guilty to simple assault last week for adhering her boyfriend's penis to his abdomen and his scrotum to his leg. Of the charges, the boyfriend commented, "I don't get it. It was consensual."

There are apologies. I make them. She makes them. I arrange for the price of her groceries to be taken out of my paycheck, which is semi-underhanded since I know I won't last another day in this place. Once this transaction is complete, she says that she should demand I be fired, but she can see that I'm a mother too. Her name's Sister, she says, like we're meeting in church and I think, What kind of name is that for a grown up?

"I wish we were meeting under different circumstances, Sister," I say.

"If it makes you feel any better, I think I'm in the middle of a nervous breakdown," she says. It does make me feel better, but I keep this information to myself.

Leslie isn't surprised when I call her again and tell her I have molested a woman in the parking lot and I need a ride because I'm too jittery to drive. "Figures," she says. While I wait, I drink something called Mountain Blast in the outdoor garden section. I'm next to the bagged mulch because it seems appropriate to my mood. Leslie's car is easy to spot: black and sleek, the kind of car female assassins drive. I know she won't let me drink the Mountain Blast on her leather seats, so I settle it in the hands of a plump garden gnome and leave this job forever.

"Did you hear about Mary Tyler Moore's house?" she says, as she shifts into gear.

"I don't want to talk about it," I say.

"Oh, I think you do want to talk about it. They're asking two million. Million, Jules."

"She never actually lived there, you know. They just used it on the show."

"It's probably a shithole anyway. In real life, I mean."

"Probably a total fucking shithole. Just goes to show you."

"Yeah."

I've never felt so tiny and mean in my life, so cowed by the realization that I might be terrible at being a person. There is no herbal remedy for that. "I never even watched that show," I say.

"Me either."

"I don't know why we're talking about it if we've never seen the show." My voice is high. Too high. It's never been this high with Leslie before. I don't know if our friendship can handle my high voice.

"Look," she says. "Tell me what to say, and I'll say it."

I walk in and Ray and May are right there at the kitchen table—arranged and silent, like they're in a window display for domestic tranquility. Automaton Ray lifts a glass of water to his lips. Automaton May moves her legs like she's in a swing. I unzip my vest and hang it on the doorknob. The automatons look at me. They smile.

"Well?" says Ray. "How'd it go?"

"Were you waiting for me?"

"Of course," says Ray.

"Why?"

"We made dinner for you," says May.

There's a red-striped bucket of chicken on the table. Ray shakes it at me, and the parts move and scratch inside. The scent feels as thick as grease. I take three plates from the cabinet and hand them to Ray. I take the roll of paper towels from the spool and stick it next to the bucket. I ask them if they're going to eat the chicken with their mouths open again.

"Yes," says Ray. "And we're going to make the bones do a dance on the table."

"Good. I love that," I say.

I pull out two legs and hand them to May. She can't handle the wings or breasts yet. Too many bones. She wants to know: did the chicken ever fly? I don't know if this is a legit question or the beginning of a joke. I tell her I think the wings are just decoration. She seems content with this answer, nodding her head over-dramatically. Ray asks me how was work and I decide I have a responsibility to tell my husband and my child that I have really lost it this time.

"I have an announcement to make," I say.

They stop eating. This is the only announcement I've ever made. I don't know what the announcement will be like. I reach, but the words aren't there.

"You're quitting your job on the first day," says Ray. He gets at the fried batter smear on his chin with his paper towel, excited by the guessing game he thinks I'm inviting him to play by taking too long to say what I want to say.

"You're sick," says May, excited too.

"You're pregnant," says Ray. "Are you pregnant?"

"No, I'm not pregnant," I say. "What is wrong with you people? I have to be pregnant to have news?" I throw my wing back in the bucket. "How could you say that?" Slowly, very slowly, I push my chair back from the table and stand. I walk to the door and open it. I walk through the door and shut it. I walk down the stairs, counting in my head. Then I'm walking down the street, counting the trees in the concrete. One every five steps. Seven on every block. Soon, I'm running. I pull the rubber band out of my hair and let the gnarl fall in my face. It's a halfhearted disguise. Everybody around here knows what I look like when I'm mad. As I run, I tell myself into a story, sew myself into the seams of somebody else's, one of May's.

I'm the woman who lives in a house made of diamonds, the woman who bathes alternately in buttermilk and chocolate. I'm the one who mends owls' wings to pass the time and knits birds fancy new nests as a hobby. The one who speaks to trees and plants and tells them all the good jokes. I run down the street, and I tell myself I'll never slow, never stop, but there's a commotion up ahead. A man has chased a woman to the bus stop, and he's hitting her with splayed fingers over the head.

"Stupid," he says. "You stupid."

He may not be hurting her—the hitting is not hard—but this is definitely one of those moments that require a decision. Are you the hero or are you the bystander? The woman in the story in my head has better things to do. She's got her diamonds to polish and her tubs to fill with molten sweets and maybe a gentleman caller or two to entertain. But maybe I've never been brave enough to be that woman. Maybe the only truly inescapable fact of my life is that I'm myself.

"Hey!" I say to the man. "*You're* stupid."

FILM FOR RADIO

The wife, Audora. We all know how irritating she can be. In her first scene, the news of the impending revolution elicits from her a petulant moan. She nearly faints. Her sallow arms flap in sleeves as wide and white as pillowcases. *The rebels will burn the estate,* she says, *they will steal our belongings. Our beautiful things.* Her bald ignorance of the political intricacies at hand is appalling. We've just seen, after all, the peasant child eating filth straight out of the pig trough. Has she not noticed the scraps on her servants' backs that pass for clothing? Has she not considered the plight of the soldiers who must fight their own brothers to protect the likes of her and for a pittance of a salary, for a failing sense of honor, duty, or country? She falls, must be carried like a giant fish to a chair where she slumps, deflated, and is fanned with an open Bible by a daughter.

Her grief is overacted, infecting the scene with a certain sinking falseness. The beautiful Italian lace waving glorious in the massive entryway seems staged suddenly. And the moustache on the incidental and nameless man in the background takes on a tilt now inexcusable. Its broom-like bristles seem suspended ineffectively on a dot of glue. We are aware, disappointingly, that this is only a film. We've been made fools by her in our believing. Which is why, perhaps, we can forgive the husband his whore in the city. We can forgive him the woman who calls him her prince, who answers the door in a torn slip, holding a mangy kitten beneath her obscene ledge of breast. *Laree*, he says, *so pleased to find you at home.* It's a joke, you know. Her home is the whorehouse. That's where she always is. We don't see them together in her bed, of course, but it isn't difficult to ascertain that the sex between them is rough. The way he pushes past her, sending the kitten shocked to the bricks, the way relations between men of his standing and women of hers seem generally to go.

The husband's confession to the priest is hollow, but surprisingly convincing. "Do you know," he says, "that my wife has given me seven children and I have never seen her navel? She crosses herself each time I kiss her in bed. She fingers the beads of the rosary between the sheets."

The priest fits his delicate spectacles to his nose, the long length of which he looks down, iconic in his disapproval. His face fills the entire screen.

"If you ask me," says Marcus, "she's the sinner."

"Hail Marys," says the priest. "And do them until you're hoarse."

This seems to please Marcus. He lights a long dark *cigarella* with a desk lighter the shape and size of an apple. "I am a vigorous man," he says.

It turns out that the priest plays a larger role than we may initially have expected. When the seven children picnic in the field, he stands on the ridge overlooking them, his black cloak flapping as though all the weather in the film has descended upon only him. He must wrestle with his umbrella, his only protection from the sun, which flaps like a bat in his hands. Beneath him the children of privilege extend their stockinged legs in wheat so bright as to appear overexposed, and beyond him troops march in dark couplets. They are not eager to meet their deaths for a flimsy cause, these men, and he understands this. And yet, the children are without malice. Can he blame them their stark white blindness? His position is symbolically difficult. Such is his lot.

There is a relationship springing up between Marcus and his sister's twenty-ish son, who has military ambitions. He will wave the red and white, he says, and we will all see who is right in the end. He is, for the most part, an over-eager fool, but this makes him the right vehicle for startling insight. On the eve of his departure for the front, Marcus takes him by the shoulders. "It is for others to fight this war," he says. "We cannot fight the change that is coming. It is upon us. The middleclass, they want our land, our positions."

"Don't you see, uncle?" says the boy. "The change will come, but nothing has to change."

Marcus acts dismissive of this notion, but he's only *acting*. He has heard the truth there. It has lodged itself already in the part of his mind that plots, that strategizes, that wins. Wheels turn in his eyes. *The boy is wise without knowing it*, he thinks, the voice-over booming as though his voice is the voice of some god. *Something must change for everything to stay as it is*. Marcus is a man of appearances. He fidgets with materials in his desk. "You're going to get yourself killed," he says. He fists a bundle of cash into his nephew's breast pocket.

"I'll be back in a month to show you I am right," says the boy, the bones in his face as fine as a bird's. Because he is beautiful, we know he will die. We know he will die because, as he bids farewell to the many members of his family, he assures them that there is no real danger in this war. He will die because he is young and wrong and the meaning of his death will be transcendent. Youth is often wrong, while also pure, and war makes men of boys, while also killing them. As he pulls away in his horse drawn carriage, he and his male servant wave at the back projection footage of the jostling country road they may never see again. His name is Alain. Perhaps it is not worth remembering his name.

The war is strange because it is Civil. It is difficult to discern the members of one force from the other, and kerchiefed women run through the streets, wailing over the deaths of their husbands and sons. If this were an ordinary sort of war, these women wouldn't be allowed on the field of battle, but in this war, the city streets are the battlefields. The war is happening in their domestic spheres, and they have a right to participate. Some of these women are angrier than others. A pack of the angrier ones chase a papal figure (not *our* priest) over rubble and dead bodies. *Catch him*, they say. *Hang him.* They reach at his face, and he beats back their hands. His skin is red as a pig's—a nice contrast to the black of his robes.

We leave the chase to witness a series of explosions. The men in red shirts seem to have better weapons. The men with scarves around their necks, some of them are fighting only with knives. They fall before they have a chance to stab anyone with them. It is shameless and senseless, this death and this dying. This slaughtering happening between neighbors. We understand the absurdity of war more profoundly when we find the papal figure hanging from his neck in an alley. His vestments move to the ground in a long and meaningful flutter. When soldiers arrive on the scene and ask the women why they have done this thing, the women cannot explain. "Our husbands are dead," they say. "Our sons are dying."

Audora lacks dimension, but she is not always wrong. In a more perfectly cast world, her wisdom would be charming rather than irritating. Look at her, her skirts pooled around her legs. She is on the bedroom floor, sorting through her more precious of belongings. Her glassy diamonds and gold combs. So beautiful they are, and behind each one a story. "This broach," she says, "was given to me by my grandmother on my wedding day. It can also be worn as a hairpiece or a necklace. It was her favorite of objects and she gave it to me, telling me my life would be a hard one at times and that I should always remember beauty." The pearls, she has begun to unstring already. She is sewing them into her husband's jackets. The jewels, she will uproot like teeth from their settings and hide in a little bag she carries on her upper thigh. She hopes aloud that this small gesture of caution will ensure the survival of her children, even if she herself does not survive. There is no one in the room to witness her pain. If there were, we might feel more comfortable having listened.

It is not surprising that Marcus too has a few tricks up his sleeve. He is selling his properties as quickly as he can to the middleclass merchants who have hounded him for years, properties that they could simply take from him in the coming months of war, if they were thinking straight, the fools. He sells the land cheaply and jovially to men in loud poofs of pants, men whose homes and horses say *new money* and *merchant class*. They don't yet know how to manage the respect and awe they've been raised to feel for men like Marcus. He's royalty of a sort, and they forget his insults. They look down as he unfolds hankies of almost transparent silk on their chairs so that he might sit without fear of dirtying his beautiful clothes.

They are not without a certain appeal, these minor characters. All of them are young and clearly ambitious. Their faces turn and dart with the bright inflection in their voices. No hint of pomp in their clean city accents. They are the new world. The future has been waiting for them. Their wives cleave to them while serving wine and oranges to Marcus directly. No servants. Can you imagine? Marcus can't. He is, to say the least, taken aback. His eyebrows seem unhinged from his face. There is an intimacy and a casual air between these couples that a man like Marcus would envy. He eyes the hem of a plump wife's dress, perhaps imagining it flung violently above her round head.

"Do you have any wine?" he says, as he sets his glass, clearly quite full, on a fresh, curling contract.

"Why, you're drinking a glass of wine," says the merchant. He turns subtly to his wife as if to say, what's the joke here?

"I see," says Marcus. "Do you have, then, any other wine?"

"Of course, of course."

The man sends his wife to the cellar, where she sighs in front of a dusty rack of bottles. "Drunk's a drunk's a drunk," she says, and then we enter a montage of merchant wives, standing before dusty racks, shaking their heads. A gold pen bleeds Marcus's signature on a slick series of parchment papers, and glasses of wine are filled and emptied with alarming frequency. There is red in his grey beard, his mouth a slash of wet. This is a grand swirl of imagery. Non-diegetic sound: a blast laugh, hands clapping, a moan, glass breaking, an infant crying. Marcus is drunk. Dangerously, terribly drunk. He is standing in the street, in the rain, his arms spread as though attempting to embrace a wall, and he is telling a man who isn't there what his house has meant to him. "This house is my family," he says. "Every brick is infused with life. My life. My father's. My father's father's. And now, all of it is gone. I've sold it all. Where will my sons live, and what will their sons know of me?"

In this moment, we are to understand that Marcus is a person, too.

It has been a month and still no word from Alain. His mother frets as the family estate is packed into wooden carts. "What if he returns and no one is here to receive him?" she says. "What if he is wounded and needs help?" she says. "What if he is dirty and hungry?" she says. She looks out a massive window and frets. This is her sole function in the film, to fret, and she does so bloodlessly. The activity of her body is contrived and awkward. She, like almost all of the women in *The Departure of the Horses*, has very little material with which to work, and she makes the very least of it.

This is the right time, though, for love. We can feel it coming as the camera sweeps past the fretful mother's dark skirts and onto the veranda. The countryside expands, its sexuality palpable, as we move into the garden, which opens itself fluidly. The trees can't contain their cleavage. There they are, the lovers, in the deep pocket of the flowering orchard. She is pulling a dogwood's felt around her shoulders and he is turning a tick of flowers like tiny kitted bells beneath her chin. We can see by the way she's dressed that she's the one with the money. One of Marcus's daughters. We've seen her around. Earlier, she helped to carry her swooning mother to a chair. She may have been in something else too, a larger role, one with more grit to it. She's one of those actresses with potential who shot off too soon.

He is a boxy sort, although not unattractive. His largeness suggests something of the farm, as do his clothes: leather slacks and vest, a billowy linen blouse. He is wholesome, a heart of gold, and their love is a forbidden one. She says that her father would never approve if he found them there. "He'd send me to the convent," she says, repeating what they must already know. And he tells her, moving behind to take her bone-thin shoulders in his oversized hands, that times are changing. "It is true today that your father owns as little land as I do," he says.

"You mean we could be together?" she says, her face lit bright like a spot of moon.

"Listen to me," he says. "When all of this is over, you will be my wife."

Their kiss is passionate and gauzy, almost perfectly drawn. It brings to mind the idea that some human bodies have the capacity to fit together so well as to be impossibly matched. And there in the distance, where you can barely see him, is a grip in a black jumpsuit. He is holding a boom.

The dog is a mastiff. It appears most frequently in outdoor scenes, although it also appears quite fond of the foyer. It likes to be at the door when people arrive, and it likes to take Marcus's hand into its giant mouth as though simply to hold it as they walk along together. The dog will be a sacrifice of the move. Having never left the estate, it will not understand the call to follow. It will go as far as the gate, and that is all. Perhaps it will become a middleclass dog and never know the difference.

A word about the dust: it is *everywhere*. The journey into exile is a dirty one, but as far as Marcus is concerned, it's OK. He has hunted all his life, after all. He is an expert equestrian and has the capacity to shoot tiny birds off posts at long range. His wife, however, is a disaster. A rare moment of comedy occurs when she resigns to winding her entire head in her shawl, while sitting atop a large fake horse. "This wind is miserable," she says. She must shout in order to be heard.

"If it were not for this wind, you would be smelling the stink of the hogs," says Marcus. Awkward stock footage of hogs rooting beside a dirt road follows, the quality of the film grainy and the colors strangely poppy.

The seven children are driven in fake-horse drawn carts that follow their parents' fake horses, and behind them, the various minor familial characters and devoted servants trail. It is not clear exactly where they are headed, only that they are going and that they must go in order to avoid sure persecution as loyalists. One of Marcus's daughters is weeping hysterically, and he can't figure her. We know, though, that she is in love and our knowledge is of a pleasing kind. *We know something Marcus doesn't know.* The fretful mother is also weeping, though silently. Her shoulders spasm in the black lace she has taken to wearing which seems to connote her resignation to the idea that her son is dead. This only serves to confirm our sense of his impending death; it's jackhammered foreshadowing. We are feeling less and less smart all the time about our predictions. The smallest of Marcus's children is asking about the dog. Over and over again, he asks about the dog and is ignored. His tiny feet dangle out the back of the cart.

The family is welcomed into a stone pavilion by a man in very formal attire. The brief exchanges between Marcus and this man are merely informational. We learn that he is a man of Marcus's standing who lives far away enough from the fray to feel safe for the time being. The priest meets the family as they spend their first night away from home. He is ushered into a room by a servant named Bepe and is shocked to discover Marcus emerging from a bath. His skin is pinked by the heat of the water and white suds stream down his body. His nudity is disconcerting. Jesus, but he is beautiful.

"Forgive me," says the priest. "I did not know you were bathing."

Marcus seems annoyed, though unembarrassed. His shoulders are squared and his face is in a fist. "Hand me that towel," he says.

The priest is flushed and confused. The towel is clearly within Marcus's reach. Sidestepping the bath, his eyes averted, the priest pulls the towel from the rack and extends it cautiously to Marcus. There is a pause in which it seems as though Marcus may do nothing, he might stand for hours and drip, and then he leans to take the priest by the neck and pull him to his chest. He sniffs the priest's head and underarms. "Take my advice," he says, "have a bath occasionally."

The priest pushes past Marcus, makes to leave the room, but stops at the door and turns as though prepared to say something less than priestly. His hands go up and then they go down.

"You are my only friend," says Marcus. "It is true, you know." He stands in his bath and drips.

Marcus and Audora. They are in bed. She is holding a white cloth to her mouth and crying into it. "We should sleep," he says. She shakes her head behind the cloth.

"Try to sleep," he says. She shakes her head again. What a peach she is. Attempting to console her, Marcus kisses her lightly through the cloth. "Sleep," he says. As he pulls the blankets to his chest and turns his back, she crosses herself vigorously and winds her rosary around her wrists. In a voice so loud that it bends into a static roar, Marcus tells her again to sleep.

We might feel bad for Marcus. He *has* lost all of his land, he's facing a new world order, the war is raging, his favorite nephew is probably dead, he's lonely, and he has no place now to take his entirely warranted sexual frustration, but he is an abrasive sort. It's a fine line he's walking now. There he is, riling everyone out of bed at five in the morning—the town bells have just rung him out of his sheets—so that the family can attend the early mass before they hit the road. "But father," we want one of the seven children to say, "we are fleeing death at the hands of rebels who resent our wealth and standing. Can't we skip church just this once?" Not one of them complains, though. "Get up," he says. He says this into their ears and their faces. "Get up, get up, get up." And they all wordlessly comply, tromping zombie-like to their washstands.

The scene in the church seems out of place until we understand its visual significance. The *mise-en-scene* is God and all his glory. Jesus and a thousand golden angels, Mary and her robes of baby blue so simple and so pure, Marcus's family all knees to the parquetry without the luxury of any padding or pews. The church itself is massive, and its walls are built of some old and dark stone with a reddish hue. Candles flicker and a priest (not *our* priest) raises his hand to speak just as, in the background, a dozen or so beautiful brown horses gallop past a door shaped like an upside-down horseshoe. Outside, the sky is a brilliant blue, and the horses race up a hill as though attempting to meet this color, to be enveloped by it. This, we realize, is the departure of the horses of the film's title. The religious and political implications are there, we feel them, but what the hell are they?

The music swells as we fade out and into a travel scene identical to the last, only the horses are real this time, and we can see up ahead that there's a pack of red-shirted soldiers mulling around a barricade in the road they've built of wooden debris. "Let me do the talking," says Marcus, as though there would be any argument. He swings from his horse fluidly and pulls a hunting rifle from his saddle. The soldiers approach him with their hands held out, as though to say either *hold up*, or *we come in peace*. Hard to say. A man in a uniform more uniform-ish than the rest moves forward and in a pompous air says, "Your papers please?" He hangs on the 'S' of *please*, drawing it into a hiss. Marcus turns to take in his herd of family and hangers-on (they are looking at each other worriedly) and pulls a folded sheaf of papers from his breast pocket. The man hardly glances at the papers before proclaiming to the group, "You cannot pass." Anger is swelling in Marcus's face. A man more savvy might negotiate with the pompous soldier. He might offer him some cash. But Marcus is not savvy. He is angry. "Do you know who I am?" he says, his chest arranged in a bold puff.

"You could be the king of France," says the pompous soldier, "and I still wouldn't let you pass."

"I am Marcus, head of the family of the loyal star. I demand that you let us pass."

"We are under strict orders not to let anyone pass," says the soldier. "I have the orders right here." He waves a tiny scrap of paper in the wind and beckons his troops to turn the travelers around, send them away.

"I am Marcus," says Marcus.

The troops look to Marcus and to the pompous soldier and the soldier urges them to back from whence they came. "Go on," he says. "Go on." He strikes at the dusty ground with a little horsewhip and it looks as though Marcus may be defeated. He has no little whip. "I am Marcus," he says. No one listens. What will happen if the family has to go back? Will they be killed? Knifed? Will they be forced into labor that embarrasses them? That would be depressing. Marcus makes to rifle-butt a soldier tugging reigns away from Audora—she is moaning the moan again—and a struggle ensues. Marcus is fighting for his life on a literal, as well as symbolic level. He is twisting the pompous soldier into a headlock that looks impossible to break as two soldiers climb his spine, while simultaneously struggling with the various social and political forces that have aligned to destroy his life. The dirty wind is back, obscuring the scene in a brown whirl, when a rider on a bright horse appears. "Take your hands off him," says the rider. "I fought with you at the battle of the rising crop and the slaughter of ding-high. Let them pass."

Alain. He is alive. His timing is supernaturally perfect. Or, maybe he waited like a little bitch behind the barricade, watching the whole scene unfold. The fretful mother swoons in her cart, and the daughter in love stops her love-weeping, and the little boy peaks out from beneath a sheepskin blanket. The soldiers allow the family to pass. We watch them breach the barricade from an aerial perspective, as though we are passengers on the back of a giant soaring eagle.

Alain now wears a black band around his head. It conceals his apparently mauled and sightless eye. So proud is he of this wound that we begin to suspect we are meant to understand that his eye might be fine under there. The stories he tells of his days on the front are contradictory and bizarre. "You do not know fear until you have stared down the length of one of these," he says, aiming the snub barrel of his awkward pistol between his own eyes. The family, arranged around a fireplace in some sort of rustic inn, gasps a collective gasp.

"Let me see that thing," says Marcus. He snatches the pistol from his nephew's face and runs through various maneuvers that allow the bullets to spill discreetly into his sleeve. "This is not one of our guns," he says. "Where did you get it?"

"I took it from a rebel," says Alain. He looks eagerly to the faces around the fire, all satisfyingly rapt. Audora's mouth is wide enough to allow a bird inside.

"Did you?" says Marcus.

"He was alive when I took it and dead straight after," says Alain.

The story of Alain's first kill is a familiar one with a few notable exceptions. He endures the pressures of several hard days in battle, sleeping in ditches and hiding in burned-out houses and barns. He eats only what he can find, feels lucky when he discovers a half-rotten potato in the hand of a dead soldier. The rebel soldier and Alain surprise each other in some brush, they lock eyes and neither of them fire. "I don't want to kill you," says the rebel.

"I don't want to kill you either," says Alain. "What do you propose?"

"We'll walk away and never speak of it. Five steps back and then we turn and run. We never see each other again."

Alain agrees and the two of them take their five steps back. The rebel turns and runs, as they've agreed, but Alain does not turn. Instead, he shoots the boy in the back. The boy falls, his arms pulling at his back as he strains in the dirt. Alain approaches and disarms him. He then shoots the boy dead with his rebel gun.

Marcus shakes his head and hands the gun back to his nephew.

"The rebels are trusting fools," says Alain. "They are peasants, farmers some of them. Untrained. We kill them more easily than they kill us."

"This was the first man you killed, and you shot him in the back?" says Marcus.

"You have to understand this war," says Alain. "Killing is like making love or pissing. That's what they say, but then it isn't true. It's more like a cancer. The canons are a kind of language. They tell you what to do."

Marcus looks at his hands and then he looks straight up. We, suddenly, are looking straight down into the white of his eyes.

Alain sits alone beside the fire. Disturbingly, he pours a full bottle of wine over his head. He sits, slick as a newborn, and bounces the empty bottle against his shin.

The family has arrived at their final destination. We know this because Marcus announces it needlessly to the keeper of the inn, who behaves as though he expects exactly to receive this information out of nowhere. "Very well," he says. "Very good for you." He points, with an achy flourish, to a figure on a piece of paper— the bill.

"Oh, yes," says Marcus. "Of course." He pulls a stack of bills from his breast pocket and folds three back with a thumb. The innkeeper shakes his head. Marcus folds back three more bills. Again, the grey old innkeeper shakes his head. This is a classic sort of scene, though generally done in the context of a bribe. It must confuse

Marcus. His smile all teeth, he flips the entire stack onto the table. And again, the grey old innkeeper shakes his head.

"How much could rooms cost in a place like this?" says Marcus.

"Your currency's no good here," says the innkeeper. "The war, you know."

"Of course it's good. Don't be ridiculous," says Marcus, his hands hipped. And through the triangle of empty space between his left arm and his side slips a satin-gloved hand that opens. Inside the hand is a versatile bit of jewelry. It could be a broach, a necklace charm, or even a hairpiece. It is silver, and in its center is a pale blue stone. The innkeeper's hand covers the jewel and pulls it slowly away. That Audora. What would we do without her? In his heart, perhaps, Marcus feels a little flutter. Perhaps he remembers the girl that was his wife before they married. Yes, in fact we're fogging and fading into just such a scene. A young girl—we know it's Audora for the broach on her breast—she's swinging on a swing of vines in the garden. Higher and higher she swings, her long curls drawn down by the pull of the earth for her. So beautiful, she is, and smiling. See what can happen of a woman under the force of a flashback? It's like the creation of fine gems in reverse. The diamond becomes the coal under the pressure of the plot.

The priest, *our* priest, is removing his collar. He sets it deliberately in a box and kicks the box beneath his bed. He walks hard to the door and then turns, walks back to the bed. He pulls the box from beneath the bed, removes his collar from the box, and re-fastens it at his neck. "Yes," he says. "Much better."

It is morning. All are nestled within their beds. Alain emerges from his covers in full uniform. We know what he's up to. He leaves without waking anyone and returns promptly to the front. He is there in two quick cuts: he sneaks away, he gallops madly on his horse. Into the first fray he can find, he leaps valiantly as though projected by a spring from his steed. The men in red shirts like his are cornered in old horse stalls. From the other side of the wall, he speaks to them. "I'll distract them," he says, "and you take that opportunity to shoot your way out." His voice is low. It is serious. It is manly.

"Too dangerous," says a voice behind the wall. "You'll be killed."

"Yes," says Alain. "But I'll have fought. "

He chooses a wild line and runs, his arms windmilling, drawing the fire of the men with the scarves. He is shot in the back and falls, never having fired a shot himself. His head is then cradled in a bearded man's lap. We see him from above, as the man would, and still his beauty is apparent. His cheeks are dark, flecked with dirt, and his hair is matted to his head like a black cap. His eyes shine like glass. "Is there anything we can do for you?" asks the bearded man. We know what this means—that nothing can be done.

"Tell my uncle I never fired on that rebel," says Alain. "I was only just afraid to die."

It *is* right to cry in a moment like this one. The music is high, it swells in a wave of strings. The life is passing from this boy's eyes. It's apparent in the minor key. When we were younger, when we didn't have hurt of our own, this kind of hurt might have moved us. But now, but now. Now we are moving into a clamorous scene. Women in dresses constructed of nearly transparent red scarves are spinning. In their hands golden castanets ring like a cascade of doorbells. Their hips churn and whip. As the dancing and spinning becomes coherent, we see that there is a woman in a white dress of scarves at the center. She is different from the others. More beautiful, more skilled in her movements. She turns her body almost fully around before snapping her head to meet the rotation. The effect is to draw the viewer's eyes to her sultry pair, her lashes as heavy as feathers. The music softens and she begins to sing. To sing! Her song is a lilting gypsy ballad. Her lips are so red-heavy they can barely fit around the words. Her breast curves inward as the lyrics lurch into the miseries of war, and it opens wide as the song celebrates the essential spirit of all of the nation's citizenry. *We hate ourselves for our own beauty*, she sings, *and yet we are too beautiful to hate.*

Men in dark cherry shirts surround her. Their dance is a tilting sort, their bodies diagonals. Closer and closer they lean, until the singer in white is a tiny straight line in a sea of red. She hides her face in her hands, afraid of the smothering ring. Viewed from above, though, the swarm of dancers appears as a beautiful red flower, the petals made of the leaning men and at its center the soft white dress. The woman snaps back her head and her face beams. A bold and uninhibited smile and then a wild shriek. White birds are released from beneath her dresses, and they rise to meet us, the scene dissolving in the chatter of wings.

And then this, Marcus and Audora on a rooftop. The sunset lit heavy over the sea, the clouds folding in on themselves like brilliant rips of paper, and the two of them embraced in an embrace so firm as to be elemental. Below them on the beach, their daughter is embraced by her garden lover. The water is licking at her dresses. And she doesn't seem to care. Up the beach, the little boy runs with a dog, a tiny black dog, and beyond him the others splash each other with saltwater while the fretful mother scolds and scolds and, finally, limping along with the help of a crutch, the wounded Alain waves. This world goes black. And then the room is cold.

The film in this story is inspired by The Leopard (Il Gattopardo), *1963, a film co-written and directed by Luchino Visconti, and based on the novel by Giuseppe Tomasi di Lampedusa. Several of the scenes in "Film for Radio" are drawn from scenes in the film, as is the character of Marcus, played by Burt Lancaster in* The Leopard.

The Roads Are Like That

Easing up Sand Ridge, there's a hill like an Adam's apple beneath a weak chin. It's steep and sudden. You wouldn't expect such a shape in a road—you have to nurse your engine over, hope for purchase on the gravel. I've seen Cassiopeia perched there, her limbs stretched to the hill by the vertical pull of night, and I've seen a full, old moon bluing snow that seemed only inches from its bright rim. Every so often, the three Carter cows loiter at the crest, picking at Indian grass with bowed snouts, their bodies angled to the sky. You half expect them to tip, half to fly. It's such a sharp rise that the mailbox signals peril, a white three-gallon bucket, nailed to a fence post. And when headlights hit it from the opposite side, you pull to the berm out of courtesy or fear.

The police said Lodi was hit there. They stood on my porch and expressed regret read off government-issued cardboard squares. They re-seated their terrible paunches almost in unison. There would be questioning and investigating later, they said, but at this time they only wanted to speculate. In their telling, it made sense he was hit there because it had happened before, even despite the sign, the thick black line depicting the curve in a frame of rusted and scatter-shot yellow. Only a month prior, a teenaged kid lost his grip on the wheel and ran down the fence. The way they figured it, somebody came over Sand Ridge too fast, hit Lodi, panicked, and dumped his broken body back in the woods. It was a pair of hunters who'd found him there, not twenty yards from the road, his legs pulled up to his chest and his eyes closed. It could have happened to anybody, they said.

The roads are like that. You get arrogant and start trusting them not to move on you. My own head-on was with a grey-haired member of the Liar's Corner Commune up three miles from me. He swung out of the drive and stalled, paralyzed like a doe. I was singing along to Stella, *but I'm a housewife now*, and took him by the dead right eye of his Charger. *You can't have it all*, he said. *Little girl, you can't have it all*. And all he meant was the road, but I understood him as sage. The speeds out here aren't posted, and even the school buses break fifty, their wheels lifting dust that lingers high in the trees. You could imagine one of those buses or a truck taking Lodi without even realizing it. He'd be a strange pressure in the road and then nothing.

Also, they'd found his cap at the crest of the hill with blood soaked straight through. It was snagged in the barb that penned in the cows. They called it positive evidence that there had been an accident. A real killer would have been cleaner, more careful. This accidental killer had been scared. It could have been anybody or nobody and there was no way of knowing why or what had happened. But I knew more than they did. I knew that hat had been bloodied days before he'd disappeared and I knew the reason he'd gone off in the first place. When he left, he said he was going for a walk or maybe he didn't say anything and I'd only imagined he'd spoken. He left the door flung open, and when I shut it I caught sight of his tracks, sunk deep and wide, headed straight back into the woods. I could have followed them. I could have followed them for miles, maybe, and never found a thing.

Winter gets mean on everyone. The snow hit and Lodi and I weren't ready for it. A record dump on the region and a pair of idiots in the woods. We had maybe a gallon of water. I hadn't been shopping, had been wanting a piece of plywood cut to size for the loft so we could use the space for company and decided to hold the money. There were canned foods. There were breads and some clementines, their skins just beginning to pull from the fruit. We thought the roads would be clear before we'd have to tangle with the three bricks of tofu lodged in the ice loft.

It was exciting at the start, the dim peril of it. No light, no central heat, this was before cell phones and the internet was a thing only other people understood, but the telephone lines were down and that gave us a sense of full isolation. That first night we held each other in the dark and wondered if anyone in town would worry after us. Seemed unlikely. We weren't the kind of people anybody'd think about. We were the scruff the city talked about *assisting*, about *re-orienting*. The night went on with Lodi talking his romance from beneath the weight of a high stack of down comforters. He said I might as well accept him as permanent. "Accept it," he said. "I couldn't leave you if I tried."

"Have you tried?" I asked.

He pulled my hips against the knobs of his and touched his hooked nose to mine, convincing me of him, though I didn't need convincing. I knew well what we were to each other. Like symbols in separate equations. Placeholders. But he was a love talker. He went in for drama. "This is my heart here on my sleeve," he said, "right here. You can't see it in the dark, but it's there." Call it his heart that led him to his death.

Lodi and I met on the berm of the state route. I was on my hands and knees in the gravel, playing at changing a flat, like clapping hands without contact. He blew by in his Ford and nearly took off my feet at the ankles. He sent my ass skidding into the half-pegged wheel. I crawled around to the front of my blue Chevy and hung myself against a headlight in fear. I didn't notice him pull back around until his high beams shot between my knees from beneath the car. He walked around with his engine left running and didn't speak. Just stood there with his hands pulled behind the base of his neck and his lips pulled tight over his teeth and apologetic. We went to work together cranking off the rusted bolts, laughing when our hands slipped on the lever, causing us to fall into each other like kids.

He said he'd follow me home, and I drove to the bar where I work. The Smiling Saddle. He followed me right inside, and I let the bar buy us two beers. We sat and drank. Already, our hands were hunting for each other under the table.

"*Es tut mir leid*," he said. "It's German for *I'm sorry*. The only words I know."

I said, "Maybe they're all you need."

He said, "I could have killed you."

He drove me out to the fire tower in the national forest that night, and we climbed. The box was boarded up at the top so we sat on the rungs and looked out over the trees. It was verging on cold and wind swayed us on the tower. It was like the whole thing was moving beneath us, scraping quietly away from its base, and slipping its old iron legs through the trees. We were being carried along like ticks. In silence.

Close to morning, Lodi made a speech, said he was looking for me when he nearly ran me over. I said, "Out to get me," and he said, "No, no," like a little bird in a little coo, "Like fate." He said he was driving around that night for nearly three hours when he found me. He saw my bare legs, my shins on the yellow line and then he saw my face. "I knew you were the one," he said. I felt the high flap of flattery in my throat and then came the confession. His girlfriend was having a kid, and he didn't want it. He didn't want her. He said he knew that some kind of thought would occur to him, and it turned out to be me. When we talked then, it was about her, and what he should do, and then he was saying he already knew he loved me and palming his forehead.

I'm not a fool. I know love isn't a thought waiting to happen, or a force determined by some chance arrangement of planets. I know you don't say *love* and always mean it, and I know you don't always love in the same way. Lodi was a man in movement. He was coming to me to get away from somebody else. With enough momentum, a man can go on like that forever. But for some of us, the smallest blush of affection is enough to live on for some time. For some of us, love is as simple as a word like *yes*. We wove our legs tight through the rungs of the tower's ladder and decided on my place. He had to work early and he didn't want to go home to her.

"What if you had hit me?" I asked. "Would you have stopped?"

"I wouldn't have hit you," he said.

"But what if you had? Would you have stopped?"

"That is a funny question," he said. "Look at where we are. Look at what's happening." He spread his arms wide and turned at the waist. Below us was the black of

old Ohio woods and above us the black of Ohio skies.
"We've finally found each other," he said.

There is a light-headedness about not being where
you're supposed to be. Most of our second stranded day
we spent inside, trying to warm each other. We'd get
restless and go outside for as long as our skin could stand
it. Out there we threw snow and listened to the trees
shriek beneath the weight of ice. We gathered snow in
buckets for melting and pointed out queer shapes in the
woods. We found a young deer, fallen dead in its tracks.
It was so thin its ribs hung out its sides. They got that
way when the weather changed. Too many of them and
too little food. Lodi nudged its narrow face with his
boot.

"You think we'll starve up here?" he asked.

"I don't know," I said. "If we put our minds to it,
maybe."

"That's a good thing, then. You want to know why?"

I nodded inside my furry hood, though he would
have hit the punchline no matter what I'd done.

"Because we've got shit for brains," he said.

He put a chunk of ice in his mouth and chewed. This
was his outdoors variety of comedy. Indoors, he wore his
cowboy hat and increased his bow-legged swagger for
laughs. He did it up funny because of the awkwardness
between us. That was all he could do to keep it from
aching through. The source of trouble was that we
weren't together so much as we were together. We'd
been living there going on six months and hadn't spent
more than a few whole days and nights together. We
worked opposite ends. I did nights at the Smiling Saddle,
and he did days at the recycling place. Some afternoons,
when the weather was still warm enough, we sat out
together and drank. Sometimes sprawled on the roof,

trying to pitch our empties into the bin from up there. And all seemed right with the world. We did spend good time with each other, but never any good stretch of it. And so there was a new feel to being there together, stranded, and without work. We felt nervous about it. Like seeing each other naked for the first time. Like seeing each other.

That night, we got the cards out and tried to play a few rounds. Lodi hated to lose, and I hated to let him. I'd seen him flip a table over a hand gone south, though he was half-joking when he did it. He was drinking beer like there was a world of bottles out there, and we'd have only to lean into the snow to find them.

"Save one for me," I said, as he pried open a beer with his lighter.

"You worried I'm going to drink all these?" He tilted the bottle in his hand like an arrow to his chest, like, *Who, me?*

"I'm worried we're both drinkers," I said.

"Fair enough," he said. "We do both drink." He set the bottle on the table between us, delicate and fancy.

"We'll have to start rationing," I said. "They're more important than food."

"You know something funny? I've never been with a woman who drinks as much as I do."

"What about it?"

"It strikes me as odd, is all," he said. "Odd."

He lifted the top of his hard pack and slid his remaining cigarettes into the card kitty, fingered them around, counting. "You ever hear of stir crazy?" he said. "Here it is. Here's what stir crazy sounds like." And then his dry lips were on the rim of my ear and all of the air in his lungs came out in a carpeted blast, like a crowd roaring in a whisper. The crowd roared and roared.

"Like that," he said. He took my chin in his hand and turned it left and right. "You see?"

The third day after the snow hit, we decided to walk the mile to the nearest trailer, through thicket that begged us not to move. Lodi wanted to say hello to somebody. He wanted *outside contact*. The idea of seeing somebody else had him in a bright mood. He spit in his fist and extended his yellow glove. When he opened it, a little ice disk sat in the palm, something he'd grabbed off a tree or pulled from the ground and was trying to pass off as frozen spittle. "It's that cold," he said. We followed deer tracks to the utility lines, where they had cleared almost a road. It looked like a ski resort slope. If we could haul sleds, Lodi said, we could make a fortune. We could sell hot chocolate for a dollar and sell inner tubes for two. We could make a killing off this place. "Billionaires," he said. We watched the sunset drop into the snow together and smoked a Parliament with the filter torn off. Like he did and probably still would.

There was no light on in the trailer when we reached it. I remember thinking that there would be, though that wouldn't have made sense. The power was out over the whole ridge. The porch was ringed with plastic, and there was a child's bike sinking through a loose floorboard. We knocked and no one answered, walked around back and heard movement.

Lodi shouted. "Anybody home?"

"Let's just go," I said. "They don't want to be bothered."

He wasn't listening. We went around to the front of the place, laughing at the plywood cutout of a shadow man pissing black in the snow, and there was a full-boned man there, leaning on his pickup. Inside the truck was a gun rack. Three loaded rungs and the forth missing.

"Howdy," said Lodi.

The man spit into the snow. "What are you doing here?"

"Just checking out the neighborhood," said Lodi.

"Everything's fine. You should be on your way."

I was already taking my own tracks back up the drive, but Lodi persisted. He wanted to take the man by the hand in a shake that would mean shared hardship, shared territory. He wanted inside the trailer, where he'd bitch about the cold and learn first names.

"You should go now," the man said, easing the butt of the long gun up to rest around his exposed kneecap. He was the kind for whom *rape* and *trespass* meant the same. Our mere presence was a violation of the women he had bunkered inside.

"Come on," I said.

But Lodi was already leaning his upper-body in, he was already explaining. Then there was a sound across his face and blood in a thick stream on the snow. Lodi was on his knees. He looked at me and drew his glove across his chin. I made only the smallest noise, like a hiss escaping a turkey hawk.

"You should be on your way," the man said, pulling his thumb under the brim of his cap, so as to raise it slightly, so as to either mock or soften the violence. Lodi extended his glove to me, steaming and bloodied.

We walked back in silence. I could barely keep up with him, even with the weight of his wounded jaw pulling his spine into a curve. The night and the day that followed were black and cold. Lodi sat near the window, though it was cold and completely obscured by frost. He didn't sleep with me near the stove like we had the first two nights, under a pile of blankets so thick we'd lost ourselves beneath them. Melting snow to use in the toilet or to make tea kept me moving, while he sat. I can't recall a word spoken between us, beyond *yes*, beyond *no*. He guarded his wound like a hurt dog and wouldn't let me near his face. He'd been using his black cap as a compress, like a leaf flung in wet paint, and refused to clean the split in his cheek. He was ignoring it and everything, his eyes sunk back in his head. And then he was gone. He'd said something, or he hadn't. Made a noise with his throat that was a word or wasn't. I came around from the kitchen to find an open space where the bent-up aluminum of the front door should have been.

I spent two nights waiting for Lodi's return after he walked off in the snow, and I didn't sleep for worrying about what he was doing. He'd gone off hard for less. Once he stuck his fist through the open window of a little Civic when the jackasses inside called him *pretty* and bloodied a nose. He pried the wipers off and tossed them over his shoulder. Dusted his hands like a day's work done and skimmed back inside the bar. People asked me then what I was doing with Lodi. The regulars at the bar who feel they own a piece of me for all the money they put down on drinks. They wanted to know if I knew about Shelley. The other woman. The one he'd left for me. Old man half-dead with his finger in his Wild Turkey asked me if I knew he still saw her sometimes. "We've seen him over there, you know," he said. "With her."

"They've got a kid together," I said.

"Sure, but still. Doesn't bother you?"

"Not at all."

Lodi put that same man's face into a chain fence for asking him how he handled two women at once. This was the reason they called Lodi an animal at the Saddle. He had disappeared for three days then, walking down the highway, but he hadn't been hurt. There hadn't been snow. He hadn't needed a better coat. If I was going to warn anybody that Lodi was out there and that he was angry, I'd have to get somewhere with a phone that worked. At first I waited for the plows to come through, but then the car was blocked by the snow they heaped in the drive. I finally made the walk into town, stopping to squat in the slush and rest when the air became too sharp to breathe. It was a long journey and a painful one. I didn't know if I could make it back the other way. Once I reached Athens, I called the Athens police, not knowing if Millfield had any. They transferred me to Chauncey, and the operator sniffed. "They don't even have a stoplight to monitor out here, honey," she said. "Call Athens again if it's serious." She was surprised the phone lines were up anywhere, the whole region was hit so hard. The woman at the Athens Police was aggravated it was me again. "Was there foul play?" she asked.

"What do you mean by foul play?" I asked.

"I mean, was there foul play? If it's just a missing persons, I'll have to transfer you."

"Yes."

"Yes, missing persons, or yes foul play?"

"Both."

"One or the other."

"There was a gun."

There was a silence and then the line clicked over to an officer. He let slide that they had reports through the CB of gunfire up on the ridge, but it could just be some locals hunting. They sent a car to the fast food joint where I was holed up and had me in for questioning. The interrogation room doubled as a copy room with a wad of white paper smeared into ink on the floor. "Problem with the machine," the officer said. He gestured me into a chair and said he knew Lodi because he was a familiar character in this particular station. A real clown, he called him. I told him I thought Lodi was in danger. He set a tiny recorder on the table between us when I told him I thought Lodi was dangerous. I told them about the man and the trailer and the blood in the snow.

"They should start looking for him. If he hasn't already done something, he probably will," I said.

"He had a clear intent to harm?" he asked.

"He was angry."

"He's got a son with another woman, is that correct?" he asked. He said this in the way you deliver the answer to a hard riddle. "Isn't it possible he's gone back to her?"

"Can this be over now?"

I got a ride home in a sleek cruiser and I imagined it taking me to a place deep enough in the woods for people to forget me as more than a face that happened once behind a bar. And then I imagined it the other way. I imagined the cruiser driving me into a life so right I'd have my address printed on labels. Either way, though, I was still me. Behind the bones in my face were the bones of a hundred other women gone before, none of us having made it straight. None of us made it out, not one of us made good. No matter what kind of dress you put on me, I'm still that. I'm river dirt and coal dust. I'm the trash at the end of a long gravel drive. My house looked so tiny and sad as we came upon it. Inside it was everything I'd ever owned, which wasn't much. And I knew without knowing that Lodi wasn't there. Even if he had been, he wouldn't be by the time I'd marched all the way up the drive. He'd never have forgiven me for talking to the police. When I got inside, every last thing was in its place. And I started thinking about how it would be to miss somebody I'd always understood as gone.

After three nights, Lodi finally came back. After I'd been to the police, after I'd given up on wanting the sounds of his boots in the snow. I was pressing my face against the stove for its last blush of heat when I heard his trademark trudge. He tried the knob, but I'd locked the door out of sadness and fear. Then he rapped sharp on the window. "Come on," he said through the glass, "I want to show you something." I followed his shadow through the chaos of frost, past one window, and the next. His torso seemed disconnected from his legs as his figure darted by. I don't know why I opened the door, but I did. He smiled and wagged the man's long gun in my face.

"Recognize this?" he asked.

"I went to the police because I was worried about you," I said. I took two steps back and eyed the lean baseball bat behind the door.

"You went to the police? That's rich," he said. "Never thought you'd do that."

"I was worried."

"Forget it. I'm not going to hurt you. I just wanted you to see it."

He held the gun with an end in each hand and then lifted its butt to my face. "See where he got me with it?" he asked. The stock was chipped. "You know what? It's yours. I want you to have it. You should get something."

I pulled my arms into my chest, refusing his gift. "What are you going to do?" I asked.

He snorted and propped the gun against my stoop. "Now that I've taken care of business, I'm high-tailing it out of here," he said, and turned, his chest puffed out and proud.

"What did you do?"

He threw his head back and shouted, "Taught that man a lesson!"

"If you don't stop, you're not coming back."

"I'm not stopping," he said. "It was good."

I resisted the urge to tell him to at least let me attend to his face, the blood-crusted wound that was sure to be carrying an infection by now. I resisted the urge to tell him to hold on. He waved his gloved hand over his head as he trudged away. In that moment, I wanted him to look at me again and see my pain, so I kicked out the gun's perch, skittering it into the snow. He stopped and cocked his head to the side, but he never looked back. And so it was over. I went into my house and thought about how soon I'd have to go back to work. There would be less money coming in now, the roads were more or less clear, and there would be people ready to drink.

In two weeks, I was back in Athens to look at Lodi and tell them it was him. His hair was thick to his head, like somebody had greased and combed it there. Somebody who didn't know him. The gash in his face was blue, still clotted with black flecks from his hat. They had a rough sheet up to his chin, and I was glad for it. I had no wish to see more. The wounds, they said, were consistent with an auto accident through his middle. They told me he'd probably died on impact—with very little in the way of suffering. They were sorry this time. Didn't ask me about any other woman. But had no time to speculate on the possibility that the wound in his face was delivered by the same man who'd run him down. Of course, they didn't know Lodi had taken that gun. And I didn't tell them. The gun was mine now; he'd given it to me.

They had a cruiser take me home, and I edged up in my seat at the moment where Sand Ridge knots. We passed, slow, over that strange hill. The snow had melted down to scattered patches. There were no skid marks there, no signs of hesitation. If that man had killed Lodi, found him on the road and taken him down, he'd done it knowing nothing would ever be done about it. I felt this possibility, that he and I were in a conspiracy together. We were erasing a man until he never was. But then I knew that wasn't quite true. You lose sight of people without even knowing they're standing still.

There were too few people to call and too few things to pack up. I thought maybe his kid would want some of it but then I never heard back from the mother. Word was she'd moved to Columbus and then I had no way of knowing what became of them. One night in the Saddle, I heard that Lodi had taken that gun without a fight. He'd doused a small shed with a few gallons of kerosene, but he didn't light it. He pulled a mailbox down and smashed a truck's mirror with his foot. He slipped the gun from the truck's rack like a sly thief and walked away without a fight. Nobody ever said these things directly to me, but that's how news like this comes. At an angle. And you believe it because you might as well.

I walk now sometimes—like he used to do. Sometimes I walk straight back into the woods and I try to imagine where he hid himself for those days while I worried, how he must have made his body howl to leave it in the cold so long as he took his sad revenge. And it gets me. It makes the bones in my chest ache for the bald futility of it all. When I make my walks at night, I can go a half-mile back behind the house and still see the kitchen light when I stop. I stand there, almost wanting to see someone moving inside, something out of place happening, and be helpless to help it, be helpless to tell the person inside that the heat won't last, that he should find some other place to squat, because the winter is long, and there is wood to be chopped, much to be done if he wants to sleep without pain. There is an art to splitting wood. You have to let something of yourself go, and strike without doubt, because it is necessary, because there is no one else. Lodi told me the trick of it, to swing your palm up on the neck of the axe in one motion, like a one-syllable word, he said, like *want*, like I want this, and it will happen.

ACKNOWLEDGMENTS

I have had the great fortune of a great many supporters in my writing life. I fear it's impossible to do them all justice here, but I will try my level best:

First of all, thanks to Nick Courtright and Kyle McCord of Gold Wake Press for finding the book inside the book and bringing it to the world in this beautiful package. Thanks also to Amber Estes Thieneman, whose remarkable photography adorns the cover.

I'd also like to thank the editors of the following journals, in which versions of these stories first appeared: *Ninth Letter*: "The Art Professor's Guide to Mystical Pregnancy"; *A Public Space*: "The Collapse"; *Witness*: "Peek-a-Boo"; *Joyland*: "Girl Trash Noir"; *Memorious*: "Sole Survivor"; *The Southeast Review*: "What Good Are You?"; *Eureka Literary Magazine*: "Film for Radio"; *Swink Magazine*: "The Roads Are Like That."

Grants and fellowships from the following organizations have made the pursuit of my work possible: the National Endowment for the Arts, the Ohio Arts Council, the Institute of Modern Letters, and the Truman Capote fellowship program.

I first found institutional support at Ohio University, where the instruction of Darrell Spencer and Joan Connor were invaluable. Life-altering creative sustenance came by way of the good people at the Iowa Writers' Workshop. In particular, I'd like to thank Marilynne Robinson, Chris Offutt, James Hynes, and Thisbe Nissen for their mentorship. I'd be remiss if I didn't thank Deb West, Jan Zenisek, Connie Brothers, and the late Frank Conroy for making me feel at home. When I needed revival and renewal, I found it at the University of Cincinnati. Leah Stewart, Michael Griffith, Chris Bachelder, and Jim Schiff encouraged me to reach. My friends and colleagues at the University of Louisville are bright lights; I cherish them.

To my writer friends, who have always been willing to read a draft, I owe eternal service as an extra pair of eyeballs. In order of era, they are: Katherine Furler, Tracey Knapp, Ashley Capps, Melissa Tuckey, Anna Solomon, Lisa Srisuro, Roderic Crooks, Liz Countryman, and Jenn Fawkes.

To my parents, Robert and Jennifer, I owe thanks for a lifetime of faith and an infinite number of stories to tell. To my brothers, Bob and John: thank you for reminding me to laugh. Without my sister, Vanessa Phelan, there would be no one on the other end of my texts to encourage me to persist. Thanks also to the O'Connell, Stansel, and Lando crews; Brooke Lando is a rare gem.

And, finally, to my wonderful husband, Ian Stansel, and my daughters, Simone and Lila Lulu, I owe it all. This book would not have been possible without you; I would not be possible without you. Let's continue arguing about who loves whom more forever.

ABOUT GOLD WAKE PRESS

Gold Wake Press, an independent publisher, is curated by Nick Courtright and Kyle McCord. All Gold Wake titles are available at amazon.com, barnesandnoble.com, and via order from your local bookstore. Learn more at goldwake.com.

Available Titles:

Andy Briseño's *Down and Out*
Talia Bloch's *Inheritance*
Eileen G'Sell's *Life After Rugby*
Erin Stalcup's *Every Living Species*
Glenn Shaheen's *Carnivalia*
Frances Cannon's *The High and Lows of Shapeshift Ma and Big-Little Frank*
Justin Bigos' *Mad River*
Kelly Magee's *The Neighborhood*
Kyle Flak's *I Am Sorry for Everything in the Whole Entire Universe*
David Wojciechowski's *Dreams I Never Told You & Letters I Never Sent*

Keith Montesano's *Housefire Elegies*
Mary Quade's *Local Extinctions*
Adam Crittenden's *Blood Eagle*
Lesley Jenike's *Holy Island*
Mary Buchinger Bodwell's *Aerialist*
Becca J. R. Lachman's *Other Acreage*
Joshua Butts' *New to the Lost Coast*
Tasha Cotter's *Some Churches*
Hannah Stephenson's *In the Kettle, the Shriek*
Nick Courtright's *Let There Be Light*
Kyle McCord's *You Are Indeed an Elk, but This Is Not the Forest You Were Born to Graze*
Kathleen Rooney's *Robinson Alone*
Erin Elizabeth Smith's *The Naming of Strays*

About Sarah Anne Strickley

Sarah Anne Strickley is a recipient of a National Endowment for the Arts Creative Writing Fellowship, an Ohio Arts Grant, a Glenn Schaeffer Award, and other honors. Her stories and essays have appeared in *Oxford American*, *A Public Space*, *Witness*, *Harvard Review*, *The Normal School*, *Ninth Letter*, and elsewhere. She's a graduate of the Iowa Writers' Workshop and earned her Ph.D. from the University of Cincinnati. She teaches creative writing and serves as the faculty editor of *Miracle Monocle* at the University of Louisville.

CPSIA information can be obtained
at www.ICGtesting.com
Printed in the USA
FFOW02n0019230518
46841288-49027FF